The Search for Steam

The Frisco's 4200 class Mikados were never adequately covered in action photography. Because their operations were confined to the sparsely settled and relatively poor Ozark Mountain region between Kansas City, Mo., and Birmingham, Ala., few of the local population had either the equipment or the inclination to preserve the big Mikes' passage. Yet how could all of the far-traveling rail buffs, who crisscrossed the nation in search of steam, have missed a journey to the Ozarks to film these elusive and aesthetic machines at work?

Second only to the G.N.'s massive 0-8 class Mikados for weight and size, these Frisco machines were highly touted by many writers, whose articles suffered from a lack of smoky action, being illustrated with only engine stills. The fault may be excused, for the author has traveled, written and telephoned, seeking some scene of a 4200 class Mike pounding down the main, but there was nothing, anywhere. It remained, therefore, for famed railway artist Howard Fogg to create this rare view of a 4200, breasting a rise with a Frisco Faster Freight in Indian summer.

The Search for Steam

a cavalcade of smoky action in steam by
the greatest railroad photographers

by JOE G. COLLIAS

Howell
-North
Books

BERKELEY   CALIFORNIA

Front Endpaper

Wrapped in a shawl of its own making, the Pennsylvania Railroad's longest cross-country run, the *Spirit of St. Louis,* works up speed behind two classic K-4s Pacific types across Illinois prairies lying brown and cold under a weak December sun. (*—C. E. Prusia*)

Back Endpaper

Exhibited in the best example possible of the traditional three-quarter action pose for steam trains, Grand Trunk Western 4-8-4 No. 6333 parades through Waterford, Mich., on a cool May morning of 1958. (*—Fred Sankoff*)

Published by Howell-North Books
1050 Parker Street, Berkeley, California 94710

Contents

All pictures not credited are those taken by the Author.

The steam searcher's reward: great, gray-boilered Union Pacific 4-8-4 No. 815 shows the why of it all, racing into the setting sun across Nebraska with westbound freight. (*—Fred Sankoff*)

Foreword

The purpose of the volume in hand is to bring to light the work of both acknowledged and little-known artists in the fraternity of railroad photographers. The pictures on the following pages will, as always, tell the story of steam, a tale that all of us would hear told again and again. But also, it is hoped, this book will tell the story of the serious rail photographer. Smitten with steam at an early age, the railfan with a determination to record every locomotive on film can trace his struggles from the Depression years, when the cost of a roll of film would buy a much-needed meal; through the war years, when his motives were automatically thought to be treasonous; and into the tragic years, when the object of his love and affection was taken from him by the sudden rise of the diesel electric.

Serious rail photography was not an easy hobby — if indeed "hobby" is the right word for it. Hobbies are supposed to bring fun and relaxation, but all too often frustration and disappointment were the photographer's reward for a great deal of work. But when his efforts produced a soul-stirring, steamy portrait of his favorite subject — be it a dramatic shot of the iron horse at work or a perfectly posed engine still — then frustrations were forgotten and the urge to capture even more difficult subjects was kindled.

Men of such determination, skill and patience are as much the heroes of the age of steam as the engineers, firemen, station agents, brakemen and all the others. Without the photographers, the steam locomotive would for most of us be no more than a fast-receding memory or the dream of a golden age that once was.

Every photographer had a favorite railroad, owed allegiance to a certain part of the country, or had a pet spot out on the main line that could assure him the fantastic scenes that he craved. For Preston George, Curtis Hill on the Santa Fe through western Oklahoma was the height of railroad activity. H. Reid and August A. Thieme, Jr., chose the tidelands of Virginia for their stomping grounds, tracking the carriers of the Pocahontas coal country; and Robert Collins covered the Northeast, seeking the little-known and sometimes forgotten carriers in the Alleghenies. While the flat, open plains of Manitoba were ideally suited to Fred Sankoff's skill with the three-quarter classic pose, further to the south in the Colorado Rockies Richard Kindig established himself as a master photographer in both standard and narrow gauge. Not content to focus on one group of lines or a certain kind of topography, the late Robert J. Foster is acknowledged as *the* expert on engine stills. The author wishes to express his gratitude to these men, and the many others, for contributing their work to this volume.

Their accomplishments are all the more remarkable in view of the many difficulties encountered in a hobby that at times called for the wit and planning of a besieged general of the armies. The railroads, and especially their law-enforcement officers, were notorious in the years of steam for their antagonism toward the activities of rail photographers. Railfans suffered disdain, insult and sometimes outright arrest, all of this from an industry that should have been eager to preserve their loyalty. Few people understood the steam buff's fascination, and most often he was simply thought to be "some kind of a nut" for caring about a dirty, greasy old steam engine. In the last days of steam many railroad officials could only shake their heads in disbelief as they witnessed the hordes of nostalgic, steam-starved souls that descended upon railbuff specials and advertised final runs — any chance for one last ride behind a real steam locomotive. It is a shame that some railroad managements did not realize long ago what an army of loyal followers they had.

Sometimes photographers were granted official permission to enter railroad property, but generally it was denied. Thus the determined photographer usually had to resort to strategems that, while not really illegal, were often quite devious. At one's favorite engine terminal an advance groundwork of friendly acquaintance with the foremen and hostlers was a must. A handful of cigars ready in the shirt pocket might enlist valuable aid in engine spotting or help to obtain schedule information that was needed for planning a shot out on the main line. In foreign territory, where the photographer was unknown, resources and cunning that would make even the most modern Mata Hari jealous were brought into play: keeping the camera out of sight, or camouflaging it as a lunch bucket; wearing a hat (no operating employee in steam's day would be caught dead without headgear); never hurrying (no operating employee ever showed signs of haste, therefore anyone who did would be conspicuous). These were just the simple precautions that every photographer took if he wanted to amass a worthwhile record of a line's roster in steam. And of course there were the long drives to find just the right background for a shot, the long hours of waiting, followed by a rapid succession of steam beauties, the reward for such patience.

The search for steam was what we lived for. The layman would call it an obsession, and perhaps it was. We who were affected believed that it was contagious, and we certainly knew that it was chronic, for there was always one more locomotive to photograph, one more beautifully scenic backdrop for a moment of smoke and action with this fire-driven machine. Thank God to have lived within its lifetime!

JOE G. COLLIAS

Shrewsbury, Missouri
1972

The Hudson type, the steam locomotive whose search for immortality in man's memory and on film reached the greatest height of success, sweeps proudly and pompously over Grand Crossing and out of the St. Louis Union Station sheds in the great day of steam and heavyweight plush equipment, 1940 to be exact, with the noon departure of the *Knickerbocker*, bound for New York City. (*—Elmer L. Onstott*)

Innocents all. (*—H. D. Runey*)

1. The Innocent Years

In the beginning there was steam, and it multiplied upon the earth and was wondrous to witness. It would be forever. After all, what else was there? To be sure, a small amount of electrified railway did exist on the North American continent, mostly in the eastern United States where traffic density was just short of overwhelming. Internal combustion power? Oh, yes, McKeen and General Electric still toyed with those oddities, but they'd never graduate from the doodlebug and factory yard-goat stage. So ignore all that; steam is everywhere. These were the feelings of rail enthusiasts in the years prior to the acceptance of the upstart diesel electric as a bona fide railroad locomotive, and so, blissful in their ignorance of the iron horse's impending doom, the photographers, the students of steam and worshipers in general enjoyed their finest hour.

Steam was, in fact, so commonplace upon the American scene, so general in appearance and so taken for granted that its serious worshipers, when discovered, were oftentimes the subject of ridicule. These were the years of the engine-picture kids, those indomitable photographers bent on recording on film each and every steam locomotive in the land, a fantastic goal in view of the 51,694 locomotives roaming the far-flung rails of the North American continent. Rail photography was a rather secluded and lonely avocation generally suited to the introvert. Few, if any, publications to inform or encourage railroad photographers existed; one's own obsession and determination were the guiding factors. The cameras were folding Kodaks and subterranean-viewed Graflexes of ponderous proportions; color photography was non-existent; highways were winding two-lane affairs where a locomotive-pacing photographer was easily outdistanced by his quarry, though seldom thwarted by competitive highway traffic. On the brighter side, though, was the superabundance of that sought-after beast, the iron horse. The rail photographer's choices were unlimited, so much so that it was usual to ignore an array of smoking steam power well within camera range while waiting for one just a little more desirable, an unthinkable selectivity in today's permanent and near absolute dearth of steam power.

An all-too-commonplace habit of the human race is this failure to recognize the good in things that are generally abundant, which in turn are lamented and bemoaned when near extinct, whether they be steam locomotives, bird or anmial life, or just plain clean air. Clean air indeed! Wouldn't the pollution police have had a holiday in those gloriously smoky years of steam's reign? What self-respecting rail photographer wanted the record of a thundering iron steed without the appropriate "burning of Rome" effect billowing forth from the stack? Synonymous with steam power were the great clouds of smoke and vapor on the horizon, identifying for all the presence of steam going about its daily duties.

For many cities and towns, the steam locomotive was a way of life, at once the greatest source of both employment and entertainment. The coming and going of the trains was a daily ritual, while the arrival of a newly built or purchased group of locomotives created a flurry of excitement among the serious and occasionally interested alike. A frequent occurrence following the railroad's rejuvenation after the Depression days of darkness, the arrival of new power — always

11

larger and often in new wheel arrangements — was an event to witness: sparkling rod and valve motion, gleaming black-enameled boilers and tenders, attended to by hordes of roundhouse workers setting the pops and valve linkage, oiling newly machined surfaces, and all under the authoritative eyes of a host of Stetson-crowned officials, seldom seen outside of their downtown suites but making a rare appearance in the smoky daylight to view the new power.

The crowning moment of the event, though, was when the new power moved off the ready tracks, coupled up to its first train of manifest and highballed out onto the main iron under the admiring gaze of the onlookers, creating a spell inevitably broken with the words "Now there's a real engine!" Truly, the steam locomotive was *the* motive power in the unsuspecting and innocent years.

No glint of chrome or guttural grumble here, solid black, stained gray with soot, pure as God intended, a 4-6-2, with dust and cinders pelting the photographer, rams the Baltimore and Ohio's St. Louis-bound *National Limited's* all heavyweight consist by the Breese, Ill., depot at a hair-raising 90 miles an hour. The year is 1935, the camera is a focal-plane Graflex, and what the devil is a diesel?! (—*Walter Schaffner*)

In 1929 the *Empire Builder* rolled behind steam, and an Atlantic type at that, in Cascade green paint. The hoghead takes his ease aloft, waiting for the highball out of the St. Paul Union Terminal with the Great Northern's then pride and joy.

A few years later and the heavyweight transcontinental run was rolling behind the 80-inch drivers of one of the Big G's most famous locomotives, the S-2 4-8-4s. Resplendent with the same green paint on cylinder and boiler jackets, with chromed cylinder heads and a voluminous, all-welded cylindrical-type tender, they were a rarity on the G.N., being one of the few engines of the road not having been built with a Belpaire-style firebox, a distinguishing trademark of the most northern transcontinental's steam roster.

No. 2584 of this once proud group hides her fashionable coat of green under a more mundane coat of grime-encrusted black as she makes a rare appearance, and almost her last, wheeling a 140-car freight out of Moorhead, Minn., in 1956.

What better way to spend a Sunday morning? Be down at the station watching the hogger oil around the high drivers of the morning limited to Chicago.

The hogger of the Baltimore and Ohio's high-stepping No. 1474 has the undivided and authoritative attention of the station platform critics at Springfield, Ill., as he goes about a time-honored ritual once performed a thousand times a day across the land. As once with the arrival of the stage or the packet boat, so the loungers wait for the daily arrival of the limited, roaring to a stop on the advertised, the hoghead sliding to the ground to poke his long-snouted oil can into hidden crevices of a hot and impatient charge, the clank of the water hatch showing that the fireboy was also at work, all the while mail and express thudding sullenly onto the baggage carts, and suddenly the call to action, the twee-twee of the cab signal, saying "All aboard, highball." Impatient to be off the iron horse responds to the hogger's pull of the throttle, lunges forward, snaps its exhaust high; the long cars of peering faces roll by ever faster and recede into the distance, leaving a vacuum that only its coming on the morrow will fill.

While the memorable scene above depicts the *Abraham Lincoln* of the then B.&O.-controlled Alton Road in 1938, it also describes the Alton's own *Ann Rutledge* at left departing Springfield in 1945 behind No. 5293, one of the big crimson-and-maroon Pacifics which were a trademark of Alton limiteds on the Chicago-St. Louis run until the advent of diesel power. (*—Walter Peters*)

Ingredients for a complete roster of motive power line up on the Decatur, Ill., enginehouse leads of the Wabash Railroad. Freight, passenger and yard power are all poised for action in this starting-line portrait of heavy freight hauler No. 2705, blue-and-gold passenger speedster No. 675 and jaunty little 0-6-0 No. 543, who puts together what the others pull. (*—Walter Peters*)

Winter gets very cold in eastern Canada, and visible proof of the sub-zero temperature is clearly evident in the clouds of steam and white exhaust surrounding a New York Central 2-8-2 and a 4-8-2 getting under way out of the St. Thomas, Ont., yards in midwinter 1940. The photographer is to be commended for holding the camera steady despite cold fingers and chattering teeth.

(—*Kenneth MacDonald Collection*)

A favorite of the upper Midwest were the Milwaukee Road's 4-8-4s, and S-2 class No. 203 shows why on a Sunday morning leaving Milwaukee proper with a westbound extra. (—*Russ Porter*)

The station platform at Plymouth, Ind., is in for a dusting as one of the Pennsylvania's famed Q-2s 4-4-6-4s No. 6190, roars by at close to 60 an hour with 110 cars of westbound manifest. The unusual wheel arrangement was the Pennsylvania's last attempt at stalling the tide of dieselization, and while an eminently successful design, albeit rather unorthodox in appearance, the Q-2s retired in the face of an invasion that was based neither on speed nor power but on economics gained from areas other than motive power alone. (—Charles Ost)

For years the symbol and substance of Pennsylvania Railroad passenger train service, the classic K-4s Pacific rolled the best the Keystone system had to offer for nearly half a century. The standard passenger locomotive on the standard railroad of the world, all 425 identical machines were something to be reckoned with as regards to speed and stamina, which the competing Central and B.&O. grudgingly admitted.

A look at the finest years of steam would not be complete without a tip of the hat to America's most famous 4-6-2 locomotive, as illustrated here, departing the St. Louis terminal with the eastbound *Spirit of St. Louis*. They appeared in their later years of operation more frequently in pairs than alone, a circumstance occasioned by the increased length of the Pennsy's named trains during and after World War II.

One of the most exhilarating moments of train watching came as one stood by the switchwork at the far end of the eastside yards, in Illinois, at high noon and watched a pair of these speedsters rise out of the summer's heat, seemingly hang suspended for minutes, and then suddenly and savagely, with a bombardment of rapid-fire exhaust, explode in a blur of 90 mile an hour motion. (—Walter Peters)

Steam railroading was not all extra-fare de luxe limiteds behind speeding Hudsons or green fruit blocks following double-stacked Challengers; it was also a thousand mundane chores performed by a thousand unsung locomotives that seldom turned a wheel on the main iron. Their crews seldom received a wave from the trackside admirer as they shuffled to and fro in a world confined by the yard limits signs, but their consolation was in knowing that it all began with their efforts.

A yard crew at Kelly's Lake, Minn., bends the iron for a Great Northern 2-8-2, reporting to work for a day of probing the iron-ore pits for loads to fill out the mile-long drags destined for the docks at Superior. Behind the facade of New York-style air compressors and a footboard pilot there lurks a true U.S.R.A. heavy Mikado, grudgingly accepted by the Big G at first, but admittedly a welcome addition to the roster in the power-shortage days of World War II. (*—H. D. Runey*)

Fresh from creation and red as a newborn infant, the Illinois Central's Mountain type No. 2538 emerges from the din and dimness of the Paducah, Ky., erecting shops to face its first day of steam-breathing life. Still in its coat of protective red lead and attended to by a swarm of nurses, the newborn babe weighs in at a mere 409,500 pounds. The year is 1940, and while her lifespan will be a relatively short 17 years, she will be remembered long afterwards for the shape of her forward dome. (*—Walter Peters*)

Another member of this once famous family of 4-8-2s shakes the early morning drowsiness out of Litchfield, Ill., in 1945 with a northbound drag of coal loads.

School's out, the sun is warm, the fish are biting, and what better addition to this idyllic scene than a big Chicago Great Western 2-10-4 thundering overhead on the Fox River bridge near Geneva, Ill.? The C.G.W. shook up midwestern steam admirers in 1930 by introducing 36 of these big and, for the corn belt region, new wheel arrangements on rails which previously had supported nothing heavier than a 2-8-2.

Photographic coverage of the new machines did not equal their proportions, however, as few photographers adequately recorded their thundering activities, save perhaps one. In Jim Konas of Chicago these superpower pullers found a true admirer, a photographer and modeler who many times opened his camera lens to 2-10-4 action. Justi-

fiable reasons for such adulation are visibly present in this lordly pose of No. 867 awaiting assignment at Oelwein, Iowa, in the summer of 1948.

A relative unknown in motive power circles before the arrival of the 2-10-4s, the corn belt carrier dabbled in both oddities and incongruities during steam's reign and could at one time boast of moving much of its freight tonnage behind a fleet of 70 Prairie types, the largest wheel arrangement on the roster. Veteran Prairie No. 276 may not work as hard, but the hours are just as long in peddler freight assignments as she spends her days of semi-retirement working the local past the C.&N.W. tower at Mankato, Minn., as shown here.

James Konas (above and top left)
Charles Ost (at left below)

Idol of boyhood, in the most respected of professions, lord and master of the iron horse was the steam locomotive driver. What boy didn't look up at those cab windows and aspire to that position of magnificence, at least once in his early life. The master on his throne he was, in this case a Frisco Railroad hogger robed in denim easing his big 4-8-2 charge into a suburban station stop near St. Louis before heading into the night and the Ozarks with the *Texas Special.* (—Wayne Leeman)

Ghostly in the glare of yard floodlights, Colorado and Southern 2-10-2 No. 900 waits for the car toad to take down the blue flags on a string of northbound freight in the Denver yards. High-mounted headlights on antiseptic white, flat-faced smokebox fronts were long a trade-mark of the Burlington and its subsidiary steam power. (—Richard Wallin)

Steel and timber combine to give aerial flight to Canadian National Mikado No. 3596 rolling an eastbound extra over the high bridge at Rivers, Manitoba. (—*William Kuba*)

Out of the passing track and onto the main comes Illinois Central 2-8-4 No. 8018 with 120 empty, red company hopper cars running as second No. 71 south. It is a hot August afternoon and the hogger, after waiting for several northbound redballs to pass, is working the big Berkshire into motion with a vengeance.

That winter is cold, windy, wet and altogether miserable is no news to a Chicagoan, except perhaps to a well-insulated rail photographer to whom winter means swirling snow, billowing white exhausts and stark white backgrounds for the black bulk of a steamer at work. The price of it all is cold feet, red noses, numbing fingers and ears, yet the reward is often well worth the self-inflicted torture. Enjoy in comfort, if you will, a Chicago and North Western R-1 Ten-Wheeler stamping its feet in the snow at Arlington Park, Ill., and nearly hiding its Christmas mail extra in a cloud of leaking steam and swirling snow.

On just about as miserable a winter day as the Windy City can muster, a New York Central Niagara swings into Englewood Station.

Charles Ost (above)
Milton Nafus (at right)

One hundred fifty-five empty boxcars for grain loading in the wheat fields of Montana are rolling fast over the broad expanse of western Nebraska behind Burlington's great 0-5b Northern No. 5627. Acknowledged as the "Q's" finest in steam the robust 4-8-4s were equally at home whipping a 20-car heavyweight limited up to 80 an hour, rolling perishables at 70 per or giving the hoboes in a string of empties such as this second thoughts about their profession.

What the open hearth hath wrought: steel on steel. A Baltimore and Ohio Mallet moves fuel to the furnaces of its birth, and eventually of its death.

Rock Island was a road of questionable intent, quick to grab the infant diesel electric to power its fleet of *Rocket* streamliners, yet thereafter remaining content to let its fleet of well-maintained steam power continue to dominate in both long-distance varnish and freight hauls until well after World War II. Rock Island in steam was a beautiful carrier. The reason would be difficult to put into words but is aptly illustrated here by two of the road's more impressive locomotive designs: 4-8-4 No. 5054 working up speed out of the Silvis, Ill., yards with a westbound string of reefer "MTs," while a K-68 Mikado follows vainly behind as the second section. (*—Charles Ost*)

The Soo was a gentle carrier in steam, its motive power appearing almost to ask for affection. Perhaps it was the large, canted herald upon the glossy black tender sides, giving instant identification, or perhaps more importantly, as with many a more diminutive first-class road, the roster of locomotives was small enough to warrant an almost personal knowledge of each. The wine-red livery of its passenger consist only aided and abetted the feeling.

Pacific type No. 735 and the four cars of No. 1 exiting Fond du Lac, Wis., on the Chicago-Twin Cities run in 1950 provide an apt example of the pleasure once felt by those witnessing the Soo at trackside.
(—Charles Ost)
(Lower picture H. D. Runey)

(Above) Mention the New York Central of steam years and visions run rampant of Hudsons racing the *Century* up the namesake Hudson, or Niagaras scooping water from track pans. But as with others of such illustrious reputation, this eastern giant had its share of off-the-beaten-path branches where relics of yesteryear's steam roster went their obscure, senior-citizen way. Far from the busy four-track right of way, and yet with its own method of picking up water on the fly (in the form of an auxiliary water car, a rarity on the Central), veteran Ten-Wheeler No. 1290 has perhaps seen its better days as it wheels a daily mixed over the St. Clair subdivision near Kimballs, Ont., in October, 1956, on the "oil line" from St. Thomas to Petrolia and Oil City. (*—Fred Sankoff*)

At *left* in a mixed media of motive power, all burning oil in their own way, steam and diesel alike top the grade at Minnedosa, Manitoba, with a lengthy load of stock and produce headed for the always demanding markets of the eastern provinces. The lead engine is a 2-10-0 while the pusher is a 2-8-0. Judging from the number of cabooses surrounding the pusher, there is a rear-end crew for each head-end crew on this Canadian Pacific drag. (*—William Kuba*)

Transition of a songbird. Not only pre-diesel and pre-Hudson but pre-Pacific in this 1940 scene, the Wabash's St. Louis-Chicago *Bluebird* wings its way north behind the 84-inch drivers of Atlantic No. 614. The high-striding little speedster is working up to a 70 an hour gait under the Illinois Terminal electric line overpass at Mitchell, Ill., with six heavyweights, the absolute limit of its consist if the blue-painted flyer is to stay on schedule.

The addition of air-conditioning equipment to such consists brought an end to the 4-4-2s of Wabash ballast-scorching fame, their replacements being the more muscular yet shorter-legged 4-6-2s, as No. 673 shown here,

at left above. It is resplendent in glossy blue paint, gold trim and lettering, and chrome-plated cylinder heads, departing the St. Louis area in a cloud of dust and smoke with a heavier yet cooler *Bluebird*. (—*Walter Schaffner*)

In bright new feathers the newly streamlined and diesel-powered *Bluebird* wings proudly through west St. Louis on its maiden voyage in 1950. The ultimate in passenger finery on the St. Louis-Chicago run, the new *Bluebird* was the culmination of first wooden, then steel and air-conditioned equipment, of Atlantic, Pacific and then Hudson steam engines, all adding their share of fame and speed to this flyer of the Midwest.

2.   *The Diesel Fad*

"They'll never last! Nothing can outpull or outrun steam." Or, "Hey, look, a diesel!" Not so long ago, as time goes, these were the inevitable mouthings heard whenever that insolent upstart, the diesel electric, dared to put its foot — or more correctly, wheels — upon rails where only the iron horse had trod for over a century. Enter the diesel era, and enter it did. In an industry where conservatism was the byword, the end result of complete dieselization was a surprise as startling as the first appearance of a test unit on an all-too-familiar train through one's own home town.

Viewing the diesel as more of a curiosity than a threat, those who would in later years curse its existence hurried to trackside for a look at this newfangled gadget before it went the way of all such absurdities in the face of steam and smoke. We watched with curiosity and with some sarcasm as this carrier or that put a new offering of internal combustion power to the test, and we were complacent in the self-knowledge that, when the tests were over, these soulless invaders would be exiled to the boneyard. However, the results were spelled out in economics, not in power or speed, and the diesel's score began to mount.

Still, a fad it was, and the railroads would soon wake up to their senses. "Oh, the diesels are okay on short passenger runs, but they'll never move those mile-long tonnage drags over the hill." And yet, just as Anatole Mallet went at the problem, they too moved tonnage over the hills — with more wheels!

The diesel electric had been on the American railroad scene in various forms, none too successful but all contributing in one way or another to today's total dieselization. In 1905 the Union Pacific built and operated a short-lived rail car of its own; this was followed by scores of McKeen Company motor cars with the renowned ship-prow look, aesthetically no paradigm of beauty, then or now. It took the famous exhibition tours of the Burlington's *Pioneer Zephyr* in 1933, the first diesel-powered mainline passenger train, and the quick follow-up of the Union Pacific's *City of Portland* to make anyone outside of railroad management give this muttering youngster more than a passing glance.

Until the advent of World War II, the occasional diesel-powered passenger train that came before the lens of a railroad photographer's camera was either ignored or recorded as a curiosity, but seldom with any real interest. Apprehension as to the future of the steam locomotive, which the occasional appearance of this oil-fired machine might have caused, was largely nonexistent or, if it did indeed exist, was ignored for the most part. Few photographers saw anything of interest in a machine that lacked outside motion and a thick plume of smoke to mark its going. Steam still stalked the land in quantity.

World War II and its phenomenal movement of tonnage and people added the new diesel power in greatly increasing numbers to the roster of many a system, and more importantly it added impetus to the intrusion of the diesel electric into every field of rail transport: on long and short passenger runs, in yard and switching operations and at the head end of redball tonnage freight runs. Still the threat to steam and to the all-absorbing hobby that steam had provided was ignored, largely because everything on wheels was rolling, including those steamers once

Hustling time freight up the Cumberland Valley in a setting of new-fallen snow and crisp wintry skies is the onetime standard-bearer of the Western Maryland's early diesel roster, a genuine Electro-Motive "F" unit of once familiar profile, dressed in the W.M.'s conservative and locomotivelike black with gold trim. Artist Andrew Harmantas has here captured the feeling of sheer power and authority created by this machine. To rail buffs from the transitional period when short-lived, experimental internal-combustion designs were unseating the more than century-long monopoly of the iron horse, this locomotive is remembered as the diesel that "did in" the steam regime. Those early diesels — the *Zephyr* units, the Brill cars, and the bulldog-nosed *City of Portland* — are mostly long gone now. In the years since the diesel's victory, suppliers of internal-combustion power have altered radically not only the appearance of their product but theories of operation as well. (—Andrew Harmantas)

37

condemned to scrap and the newer, more modern steam power that was being built almost as fast as the diesel-electric units.

V-J Day and the end of the conflict brought a relaxation of the security rules around railroad properties, and rail photographers returned to their old haunts only to find the scene either changed or changing. The diesel had come of age, nurtured by the needs of Mars, and was now to be reckoned with. The search for steam was on, in dead earnest and with little time to spare.

(Above) What is it? An obviously inquisitive and yet wary onlooker peers intently at the builder's plate on the Electro-Motive Division's first diesel demonstrator, which is making a station stop at Springfield, Ill., in November, 1939, with southbound No. 19, the Alton's *Ann Rutledge*. The experimental unit went across the country extolling the virtues of diesel-powered lightweight passenger trains, eventually ending up as locomotive No. 21 at the head end of the Kansas City Southern's *Southern Belle*. (—*Walter Peters*)

Reminiscent of double-heading of two steam types of incompatible design is this pairing of a veteran shovel-nosed *Zephyr* lead unit with a more conventional E.-M.D. E-7 Class B unit diesel. This lash-up was practiced by the Burlington Route for years on the head end of the *Twin Cities Zephyr*, here paused along the bank of the Mississippi at the Savannah, Ill., station platforms in 1948. That the aesthetic mismatch did little harm to the train's schedule is obvious, since for years the *Twin Cities Zephyr* was the nation's fastest scheduled passenger haul, with spurts of over 100 m.p.h. commonplace. (*Charles Kerrigan*)

(Left) Although a lineal predecessor of the U-25s, FP-45s, *Century* units and other modernistic chop-nosed diesel designs of the '60s and '70s, the Chicago Great Western's fearsome-looking motor car No. 1004 is definitely no thing of radiant beauty as it waits for an occasional and recalcitrant passenger at the Oelwein, Iowa, depot yards in 1948. Variously altered in details of pilot, forward crew windows and radiator arrangement, the nautical leanings of the McKeen Motor Car Company are still apparent in the porthole windows and a knife-shaped front end. *(—Charles Ost)*

(Below) Pioneer in transcontinental, high-speed diesel-powered passenger runs was the joint Union Pacific-Chicago and North Western's *City of Denver,* inaugurated in June, 1936, and for several years thereafter operating on one of the fastest schedules in regular service, covering the 1,048 miles between Denver and Chicago in a total elapsed time of 16 hours, a schedule that also included eight 10-minute station stops.

Going down to the station platform to watch "the streamliner" go through was a high point in the day's activities for many a rural community between the Windy City and the mile-high capital. The moment of greatest excitement was reached when the cry "Stand back, here she comes!" was heard.

Going 90 miles an hour, 2400 oil-fed horses in unit CD-07 hurtle the *City of Denver's* standard twelve-car length down the C.&N.W.'s racetrack at Geneva, Ill., in 1947. Like the steam locomotive she and her prodigy replaced, this diesel would herself be retired within a half-dozen years. *(—Charles Kerrigan)*

In a seemingly static pose that denies all indication of speed, a pair of johnny-come-latelies in the diesel-locomotive catalog, a Fairbanks-Morse A-B combination, propel the Milwaukee Road's famed *Afternoon Hiawatha* through Rondout, Ill., at 90 an hour. F.-M. made a late but futile bid for the railroad motive-power market, sold relatively few units and succumbed early to the salesmanship and productivity of the General Motors goliath. Milwaukee itself was one of the larger buyers of F.-M.'s goods, at one time owning 15 of these units. (*—Charles Kerrigan*)

Overshadowed by the glitter of the Burlington's early silver fleet and the radically painted, bright yellow speedsters of the Union Pacific, the Missouri Pacific's pair of diesel-powered *Eagles* on the St. Louis-Kansas City-Omaha run was historically as much a pioneer in diesel-powered passenger trains as the aforementioned, more publicized group. Electro-Motive's Class E-6 units, Nos. 7000 and 7001 on the carrier's roster, were delivered in 1939. They were built with porthole windows, a styling featured the length of the fledgling streamliners.

Glistening in blue and white enamel, accented with yellow trim and chrome moldings, this ancestral unit of a whole family of E units to come chants impatientiy in the early morning light, waiting to back down to the St. Louis Station for its inaugural run. (*—Missouri Pacific Lines*)

40

A pair of early birds in the diesel-powered, lightweight, streamlined passenger train progression are pictured here departing the St. Louis area in opposite directions. The Gulf, Mobile and Ohio's very first *Rebel*, a three-car articulated unit built by American Car and Foundry Company in 1935 and powered by a 600-horsepower American Locomotive Company diesel, literally scoots across the Mississippi River Bottoms near Columbia, Ill., in 1940. *(William K. Barham)*

Climbing out of the same valley several miles to the north on the Chicago run is the Illinois Central's first venture into internal combustion power, the bulldog-nosed *Green Diamond*, another unit of articulated construction.

As with all such efforts to change habits of long standing, both such trains were immediately christened by onlookers as the "worms," the "green worm" applied to the I.C. train in reference to its two-tone green color, while the *Rebel* became the "red worm" for the same reason.

(—C. E. Prusia)

Some seven years since making its tradition-shattering transcontinental freight haul between the Pacific Coast and Chicago in 1941, the Santa Fe's very first road unit diesel, No. 100, threads the switchwork of the West Joliet, Ill., yard entrance with still another Chicago-bound red-ball. With the maiden voyage of this record-making freight, steam's monopoly of some 70-odd years on western transcontinental freight runs was broken and the roundhouse doors opened en masse to a new form of motive power — a profile that would soon be as familiar as the cowcatcher and sand dome. (*—Charles Kerrigan*)

Already 44 quadruple units removed from the original pacemaking diesel electric, No. 144 is here getting an assist from staid 2-10-2 No. 3893 as together they work up speed on the desert flats near Victorville, Calif., for the Cajon Pass climb ahead. To gain more units of motive power during the war years, the Santa Fe broke up its increasing fleet of four-unit diesel electrics into groups of three. The loss of the fourth unit made mandatory the use of helpers on Cajon Pass, just as steam power had needed such assistance. The short-term disadvantage was more than offset by the increase in much-needed motive power throughout the system. (*—William K. Barham*)

The morning schedule of trains on the highly competitive St. Louis-Chicago route called for the departure of many such runs from their originating terminals within moments of each other, a circumstance that afforded moments of excitement as later two of the competing hauls would break into a neck-and-neck — or pilot-and-pilot — race on paralleling iron out on the flat Illinois prairie. Still fresh in the writer's memory is standing braced in the open window vestibule of a heavyweight coach on the Wabash's six-car *Bluebird* as the veteran Pacific up front topped the 70 mark while, only a car-length away, the infantile *Green Diamond* droaned ominously along at the same pace. The race was interrupted only by the station stop at Litchfield, where both crews worked feverishly to load and unload baggage, express and passengers. Both schedules called for an identical departure time, but there existed just north of town a crossing at grade of both lines, and the first crew into motion usually received clearance to proceed, while the slower of the two had to give way shamefacedly. The *Green Diamond* with its newfangled diesel unit was generally the first to move, since the Wabash steamer needed water, but on occasion the blue-painted Pacific spoke first, getting the high sign and the right to proceed, leaving the insolent upstart to idle its motors in indignation. Cheers and victorious laughter would be heard throughout the *Bluebird's* consist, from crew and passengers alike.

World War II is two years past and the determined rush by American railroads toward complete dieselization has begun in earnest. The impressive line-up of departing late-afternoon name trains at the New York Central's LaSalle Street Station in Chicago no longer finds the mighty Hudson types in command. While the *Wolverine* waits its turn, headed by the idling engines of E-7 No. 4025, the *New England States* departs behind the growl of three units of F-3 No. 3500.

That the transition was not complete in this 1947 scene, as indeed it would not be for some seven years hence, was evidenced a few minutes later, as the very locomotive for which the New York Central is best remembered, a Hudson type No. 5418, updated with a 14-wheel centipede tender and a mixture of Scullin disc and Baldwin boxpok drivers, steps out of the shadows of the umbrella sheds with the eastbound *Pacemaker*. (—*Charles Kerrigan*)

44

"The diesel electric most like a steam locomotive" is the title conferred on the American Locomotive Company's long-snouted PA class passenger units by rail enthusiasts sharing a love of both forms of motive power. Whether it was a guttural exhaust that seemingly resonated in sympathy with a true locomotive stack beat, or the voluminous clouds of exhaust smoke expelled on starting, reminiscent of a Big Boy assaulting Sherman Hill, the reason for such a dubious title is apparent to some railfans. It is certain, however, that any resemblance between these square-nosed growlers and a conventional steam locomotive results purely from an act of imagination, unless one perceives the rugged, massive feel of each in a general comparison. Nonetheless these units were a favorite of the rail fraternity. Although less than a dozen railroads owned and operated them, in relatively small quantities for short periods of time, they were sought out in their final years as staunchly as the purists of perfectly posed steam portraiture sought the last of the iron horse.

At right above, one of the two such units operated by the Cotton Belt Route has the St. Louis-bound *Morning Star* in tow near Cahokia, Ill., in 1950. At right below, on the railroad most associated with these particular units, a trio of PAs guide the Santa Fe's *Super Chief* on the downgrade into the division point of Chillicothe, Ill. (*—Charles Kerrigan*) At the bottom of this page a predecessor of even the PAs, Alco-GE's first generally accepted road passenger diesel unit, styled by Otto Kuhler, the needle-nosed DL-109, No. 50 on the Santa Fe, hustles the eastbound *Super Chief* out of Galesburg, Ill., in 1941 on the last lap of its cross-country journey. (*—C. E. Prusia*)

(Above) For a fair number of years after the original articulated unit was scrapped, but before the general demise of the American passenger train in the '60s, the *Green Diamond* rolled on, if in name only, as shown here powered by E.-M.D. E-7 units in a livery of chocolate brown and orange, the somewhat unusual color combination adopted for all I.C. streamliners.

Chicago and Illinois Midland 2-10-2 No. 655 is on the passing track at Cimic, Ill., to let the Chicago-bound train pass on shared iron. (—*Walter Peters*)

(Below) An A-B-A combination of F units heads into a lowering sun in mid-Illinois with Rock Island extra No. 108. Unlike their traditionally conservative approach to new products, rail carriers threw caution to the winds in their complete acceptance of General Motors' bill of goods, so much so, in fact, that for years afterward any purveyor of internal-combustion power could be assured of at least a token purchase. (—*Charles Kerrigan*)

A trio of early Baltimore and Ohio passenger units poses on the service tracks next to the St. Louis Union Station platforms awaiting assignments. It is interesting to note that, even at this early stage of passenger diesel construction, when E.-M.D. salesmen were extolling the virtues of the diesel's inherent standardization, upon close inspection all three units are already dissimilar in exterior arrangements. Notable also is the indecision of the B.&O. as to paint and trim decor. (*—Wayne Leeman*)

A late arrival that didn't make it. The Pennsylvania's tubular *Aerotrain* sweeps down the broad four-track main line near Lewistown, Pa., in mid-1955 at close to 80 an hour behind a diesel-powered General Motors' unit of space-age styling. The unit was so different in appearance from diesels of the day, not to mention the grime-encrusted M-1a Mountains still pounding the very same rails, as to identify itself with the first McKeen car intruding into a yard full of Harriman-styled steamers. The experimental train was short lived, coming at a time when railroad passenger service was reeling under the death blows of both the airlines and the interstates.

At left a live New York Central Hudson sits encircled by enemies while awaiting the call for an eastbound mail extra in the last days of steam's operations into the St. Louis Union Station. Diesel-electric power of the Katy, Cotton Belt, Nickel Plate, Pennsylvania and New York Central itself idle the hours away on the leads of the once smoke-obscured engine terminal adjacent to the station sheds. All the units have brought in overnight runs from east, west and south, and will spend the greater part of the day awaiting the departure of their outbound counterparts. (—*Walter Peters*)

Until the advent of the chop-nosed hood unit, motive-power designers, seemingly hard pressed for ways to garb a machine that stubbornly insisted on looking like a square tube, were becoming frustrated to the point of creating the grotesque. The ultimate in their efforts, before salvation in the form of later hood units, was achieved by Baldwin Westinghouse with their distinctive "shark-nose" units, in both freight and passenger lengths. The New York Central and the Pennsylvania were the largest buyers of the units; perhaps the Pennsy was swayed by the similarity of the growler's front-end profile to that of its own onetime duplex-drive T-1 steamers, on which the road's operating department had pinned its hopes for continuing steam power. The shark noses fared little better, becoming largely obsolete by the late 1950s.

Where once K-4s Pacifics and the ill-fated T-1s themselves once smoked up the skyline in Chicago, a live shark nose and a crowd of E.-M.D. successors idle endlessly between passenger assignments in 1948. (—*Charles Kerrigan*)

51

Not all shrouded steam locomotives began life in conventional form and were later subjected to deceptive disguising; some were conceived in streamlined dress and never appeared in anything but formal skirts. Of these machines, nearly all were built to power a specific name train and seldom saw service elsewhere, until downgraded by diesel power after World War II.

Chief among such designs were the A class Atlantics of 1935 and the F-7 Hudsons of 1938, built for the Milwaukee Road's famed *Hiawatha* on the Chicago-Twin Cities schedules. Both wheel arrangements were designed for cruising at 100 miles per hour, with top speeds of 120! For their daily speed exploits and the consists that they headed, these orange, maroon and gray speedsters are legendary.

Here in a deceptively static pose, F-7 Hudson No. 102 hits the century mark with the 12-car consist of the *Hi* at Golf, Ill. (—*C. E. Prusia*)

3. *Hidden Beauty*

That first streamliner, the Union Pacific's bulldog-faced M-10,000 touring the nation in February, 1934, introduced millions of Americans to an age when the terms "airflow" and "streamliner" became commonplace. As Averell Harriman, then president of the U.P., prophesied in his dedication speech upon delivery of the three-car, low-slung unit: "This will lead to the gradual re-equipment of all the passenger trains in the country." In the public fancy this, and the multitude of aerodynamic renderings that followed, were visible proofs to Americans that the railroads were indeed on the comeback trail from the Great Depression.

To capture and hold this public fancy and the inherent revenue, streamlining and air conditioning became a must. Giants such as the New York Central or Santa Fe could afford to order both in quantity, all new and luxurious, while other systems still reeling from the effects of the lean years could only refurbish older equipment and add sparkle and flash with bright paint and imaginative names.

To power these attempts at rejuvenation, steam power was invariably relied upon; the diesel electric was in its infancy and still to be tinkered with, notwithstanding a ratio cost of three-to-one were it chosen. And so entered the short-lived era of the shrouded, streamlined steam locomotive. Over a hundred locomotives were given streamlining or semistreamlining during this period of airflow worship, from whole fleets of especially designed and built units such as New York Central's *Twentieth Century Limited* Hudson types, to such one-of-a-kind loners as the Santa Fe's *Valley Flyer* or the Chicago and Eastern Illinois' *Dixie Flagler* Pacific in black and silver disguise. Carriers with money in their pockets called upon the industrial designers of the East for sophisticated shapings, while those less prosperous lines gleaned what creativity existed in their own draftsmen and shop personnel, who swaged, cut and hammered into shape shrouds and skirting of bizarre designs.

As a rule these attempts at disguise were almost uniformly unhappy. To purists and to those of us who loved the steam locomotive in its traditional form, the results were most often mediocre and insulting. As H. Stafford Bryant, Jr., states in his excellent work on locomotive design, *The Georgian Locomotive:* "The unconscious tastes of anonymous locomotive draftsmen at Baldwin, Alco and at the locomotive shops of the railroads themselves, produced far more beauty than the conscious strivings of such designers as Raymond Loewy and Otto Kuhler to dress up the steam locomotive."

Granted, at times a truly superlative design did originate, such as the Southern Pacific's Daylight class 4-8-4s or the Pennsylvania's *Jeffersonian* K-4s Pacifics. It is interesting to note that those streamliners which pleased most adhered closely to traditional locomotive design rather than attempting to disguise it. However, harsher criticism than that expressed here would be unwarranted, for aside from bringing dad and son to trackside once again to see the streamliner go by, these colorful albeit misshapen steamers did offer the rail photographer something different to record — that rare one or two of a class that demanded attention.

As passenger consists were more and more given over to diesel-electric power, attempts at streamlining the steam locomotive were abandoned. Quickly losing the status given them by a railway management conscious of public relations and now drunk with diesel fumes, these streamliners were pooled with the conventional roster.

Underneath that torpedo profile beats the heart of a K-4s, that staunch back-bone of the Pennsylvania's great fleet of passenger power for over three decades. One of four such engines stream-styled quite tastefully for the head end of the newly scheduled, all-coach streamliners *Jeffersonian* and *South Wind* in 1940, No. 5338 bears little resemblance to its creation in 1917 as a typical K-4s with slat pilot, flat smokebox front and a high-mounted, square oil headlamp. With nickel-steel cylinder heads, chrome-plated head-lamp and handrails, airflow boiler lagging with skirts allowing access to the running gear for both the viewer and maintenance personnel, plus generous trim of brilliant crimson on keystone, nameplate and tender side, these fast-stepping speedsters were a colorful and exhilarating sight as they hit the 80 an hour mark across the prairies of Indiana and Illinois, as shown here near Caseyville, Ill., in 1942. (–C. E. Prusia)

54

Brand new, shiny and symbolic of an industry about to shake off the remaining dregs of the Great Depression, a trio of American Locomotive Company-built Hudson types lines up for an official New York Central portrait at Harmon, N.Y., in 1938. Three of ten such stream-stylings specifically created for that most famous train of all, the *Twentieth Century Limited*, these locomotives were a refreshing change from the heretofore abortionistic attempts at disguising the true identity of the steam locomotive. Since their exterior arrangement was the creation of industrial designer Henry Dreyfuss, shrouding was actually kept to a minimum, with all chassis mechanism and running gear completely exposed and actually highlighted by the polished nickel-steel rods and white-painted drivers. (*—New York Central*)

PORTER

Great are the lamentations of those who watched with more than passing interest, who recall each such moment with rapture, but for whom the camera was unknown, untried or unattainable. Rarer are those who possess the ability to re-create their memories for others on canvas or paper. Talented artist Russ Porter of Milwaukee, in reminiscing over this wintry rendering, comments that he spent many years as a kid watching the great trains coming and going out of Englewood Station in Chicago but never thought to take a photograph. "Gads, what a dunderhead!"

Two of America's most famous stream-styled steam locomotives are shown pilot and pilot in this memorable view of that once-a-day *Race of the Titans,* as titled by Porter. Experimental duplex-drive T-1 No. 6111 with the Pennsylvania's *Broadway Limited* is gaining the lead while the New York Central's *Twentieth Century Limited* behind a bullet-nosed Hudson follows a scant second later. It is 3:44 p.m. on a March day in 1943, and the "kid" takes a good photograph. (—*Russ Porter*)

Despite a generous use of sheet metal curved to lunar profiles, there is little disguising the Santa Fe's smoke-belching Hudson No. 3460, slowing for a servicing stop at Chillicothe, Ill., with a main train running as the first section of the *Chief* westbound.

One of six high-pressure and high-wheeled Hudsons built new by Baldwin in 1938, and the only one of the six to be given the futuristic shroud look, No. 3460's singular design remains a mystery. Conceived and completed at a time when the Santa Fe's standard passenger car livery was a dark coach green or a two-tone gray, with the newly arrived stainless-steel-and-crimson of the *Super Chief*

streamliner rapidly taking hold, No. 3460's exotic baby blue superstructure in two shades was, in a word, incongruous. Tagged as the "Blue Goose" wherever she put in an appearance, the otherwise capable machine spent the whole of its existence in a dress totally incompatible with a railroad where all other locomotives (save an aged 4-6-2 on the *Valley Flyer* in California, on which paint sufficed in lieu of actual shrouding) conformed to an accepted Santa Fe look, a la flat smokebox front, long pointed pilot, double sand domes and unvisored headlamp. Rolling in steam right up to the last day of steam power on the Santa Fe, No. 3460 was an oddity and a mystery alike. (*—Richard Wallin Collection*)

57

It is the author's opinion that the steam locomotive was a thing of beauty by the very virtue of its unadorned shape and unveiled working motion, and any attempt at altering or disguising these basics only served to detract from this inherent beauty. A case in point was the Southern Railway's famed Class PS-4 Pacific, readily acknowledged as a high point in locomotive aesthetics, and yet even it was not excluded from the streamlining fad of the late 1930s.

Witness if you will PS-4 No. 6689, above, assigned to the Alabama Great Southern division, all apple green jacket with lettering and striping in gold leaf, chromed cylinder heads and white-trimmed running boards, waiting in the pocket at Birmingham station for the *Birmingham Special.* Could steam as such be improved upon?

Bulbous nose, chrome necktie, a circular stairwell more at ease in the mansion of a Natchez nabob, and a pilot with the appearance of an afterthought — these are the results of one attempt at improvement, when PS-4 No. 1380 was skylined and skirted for the stainless steel streamliner, *The Tennessean.* The effect is certainly flashy, and admittedly refreshing, streaking through the hills of Dixie or waiting on the leads of the Knoxville passenger terminal, as seen here. *(—Frank Ardrey)*

While the Pennsylvania was hiring Raymond Loewy to dress up four of its 23-year-old K-4s Pacifics in stream-styled garb for the newly inaugurated Chicago-Florida *South Wind* streamliner, the more conservative and less affluent Louisville and Nashville sent a pair of 1923 U.S.R.A.-design 4-6-2s through its own South Louisville shops, where comparatively more sheet metal was used with less aesthetic effect. Wide, silver-painted skirts hid air compressors and reservoirs while the usual skyline casing hid stack and domes. However, when confronted by the L.&N.'s trademark in steam, that drumhead-sized headlamp, the shop artisans evidently visualized the results of a full disguise and at that point were reconciled to a rather conservative conical effect.

Remarkably still intact, although a bit grimy, some ten years after its face lifting, No. 275 swings through Anchorage, Ky., with the southbound *Hummingbird* on the Cincinnati-Louisville run in 1950. (*—Jack Fravert*)

One that nearly got away! Photographer Kindig admits to being deceived by the rate at which this *Hiawatha* sped across his camera's view finder. The forward-leaning look is caused by the combination of an upward-moving focal plane shutter and a speeding object at right angles. In this case the speeding object is A class Atlantic No. 2, whipping nine cars of the *Hiawatha*, No. 101, past the camera lens at well over 100 miles an hour near Deerfield, Ill., in 1939.

Yes, the wheel arrangement peeking out from beneath the skirting is a real, live 4-4-2, the first such arrangement built since 1914 — and also the last — revived by the Milwaukee to become the first originally designed streamlined locomotive. At its inception the *Hiawatha* was a six-car train, and the Atlantics were designed accordingly. However, the length of the consist was soon doubled, requiring the creation of the F-7 Hudsons. Yet, to give full credit to these remarkable Atlantics, there are many photographic records of their rapid acceleration to the 100 mark with a full 12-car train. *(—Richard Kindig)*

U.P. management chose only two attempts at pleasing the public fanc when, in 1937, in order to meet the demands generated by the Golde Gate Exposition in San Francisco, the short-lived streamliner, tl *Forty-Niner,* was inaugurated. Diesel power was already on the pro erty at the head of several *City* streamliners, but internal combustio was passed by for this newest train, because of the time element i volved. Instead, a 4-6-2 and a 4-8-2 were given custom-fitted shroud in the Omaha shops and sent forth to handle the run every fifth da Emerging in a startling livery of yellow-and-brown with a generou use of red-and-silver trim, which somehow could not be reconcil with the train's own livery of neutral gray throughout, they were bo endowed with a ground-hugging, almost sluglike appearance, but th maintained schedules akin to the *City* streamliner speeds.

The train itself was discontinued in 1941, and the metamorphosis the Mountain and the Pacific was completed in 1942, when both loc motives were de-shrouded.

No. 7002, the Mountain of the pair, is shown, opposite top, in its fanc ful garb as it picks up speed with the eastbound *49er* leaving Ra lins, Wyo., in 1937. A few years later, in 1947, No. 7002 in conve tional attire and in two-tone gray, hits 60 miles an hour with tl 11 cars of the Kansas City-bound *Pony Express. (—Richard Kindig)*

To purists of the steam tradition, the less seen of the final days of steam the better. But the story would not be complete without a lasting look at how the mighty had fallen. Compare the previous photograph of famed Hudson No. 102, on page 52, racing at the head of the *Hi*, with this despondent rendering of that same beauty fallen on evil days, awaiting the executioner's torch. The target of vandals and scavengers, this once proud Hudson sat in disrepair on the edge of the Bensenville, Ill., yards for many months before eventual scrapping in 1950. (*—Charles Kerrigan*)

Unabashed in its duplicity of design, aged Pacific No. 152 accepts the attention of a group of young admirers while awaiting the high sign to depart the Milwaukee depot with the *Chippewa* in 1952. No. 152 and a sister F-3-A Pacific, No. 151, were treated to a shrouding effect much like that of the F-7 Hudsons in 1941 and assigned to the *Chippewa*, a consist of hand-me-down *Hiawatha* equipment that served the upper Michigan peninsula country. (*—Russ Porter*)

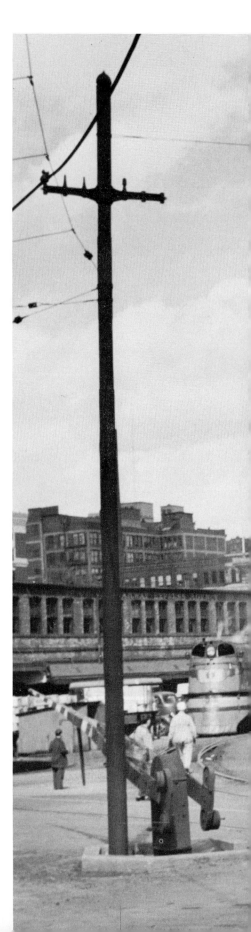

62

Who would guess that underneath that stainless-steel, shiny blue-enameled exterior of wind-splitting form and aerodynamic shape beat the heart of a 1910-built, spindly-boilered and tall-stacked 4-6-2? Typical of steam-disguising attempts of the '30s was the futuristic face lifting given to three aged steamers in the Frisco's own shops at Springfield, Mo. Students of Frisco motive power are familiar with the rather freewheeling rebuilding of the many and varied wheel arrangements on this Ozark do-it-yourself railroad. No Raymond Loewy or Otto Kuhler design these, but with a definite flair in their droop-nosed profile,

their main appeal lay in the creation of a snappy little streamliner hustling across the Kansas and Oklahoma prairies, but at a price considerably less than that of a comparable diesel-powered streamliner.

No. 1031 wheels the five cars of No. 118, the *Firefly*, the Dallas-Kansas City streamliner for which the elderly Pacifics were converted, at reduced speed through several sharp curves at Spencer, Okla., in 1947. The train itself is standard-weight equipment converted through the application of skirting, conforming roof lines and a fancy paint scheme. (*—Preston George*)

Disdaining all that aerodynamic styling or false facades of sheet metal could offer, the Alton Road instead brightened the landscape between Chicago and St. Louis with the passage of its robust Harriman-style 4-6-2s and heavyweight limiteds in a stunning livery of scarlet-and-maroon outlined in a sun-catching gold leaf. Witness, on page 14 previous, in the unfortunate limitations of black and white photography, one such colorful event.

It is to the Alton Road's credit that, after its merger with the Gulf, Mobile and Ohio and consequent dieselization, the latter carrier's management was sufficiently impressed with the steam-established color scheme to adopt it system-wide for motive power and passenger equipment alike. It is a further credit to the merged system that, as of this writing — when the intricate and ornate color schemes, which once flourished on newly arrived diesel motive power and passenger consists, have all but vanished in the face of more austere, economical and drab protective coatings — the G.M.&O.'s limiteds still depart the station sheds of Chicago and St. Louis in this onetime steam attire. Shortly after the merger of the two systems, a pair of F units in the gaudy red-and-gold trim wrap the *Alton Limited* around one leg of the twin wyes of the St. Louis Union Station at the start of the noon run to Chicago.

Beauty and the beast, but which is which? Doubtless the designers of the Pennsylvania's singular Q-1 4-6-4-4, reposing in Chicago's 59th Street yards, would point with pride to their creation, but it is safe to say that in a popular vote No. 8699, the cherub of an 0-6-0 standing alongside, would win hands down.

The Pennsy's first attempt in its much heralded and ill-fated duplex-drive concept, No. 6130 exited the Altoona shops in 1942 with this sporty dress, reminiscent of the first streamlining job on K-4s No. 3768 in 1936. With their quiet, sledge-hammer efficiency, the maintenance people had their way, and by 1945 all that remained of No. 6130's sheet-metal work were the air-pump shields and skyline contour. (—*Charles Kerrigan*)

Exceptions to specialized streamliner assignments were the nine Class E-4 Hudsons of the Chicago and North Western, delivered in 1938 and ostensibly purchased to compete with the Milwaukee's F-7s on the Chicago-Twin Cities *Hi* streamliners. Not so, said the mechanical department and promptly put all to work hauling the heavy consists of the Los Angeles and San Francisco *Challengers*, the *Pacific Limited, Overland Limited* and *Fast Mail* between Chicago and Omaha on the Galena and Iowa divisions.

An E in action was quite a sight: the towering, unbroken lines of its olive green shovel nose, propelled by 84-inch boxpok drivers, seemed to engulf the rails as it approached rather than to be riding on them. No. 4006, still in relatively decent shape in 1948, cracks the whip with the eastbound San Francisco *Overland* at close to 80 an hour near Winfield, Ill. (—*Charles Ost*)

In nearly brand-new dress, only days off the builder's erecting floor, No. 4001 steams impatiently in the cool sun of a winter's day, waiting to highball out of the North Western depot in Chicago with westbound varnish. (—*C&NW Railway*)

66

Above: Probably the most tasteful shrouding of a conventionally designed steam locomotive was achieved by the Baltimore and Ohio in 1946 when it inaugurated the Baltimore and Washington, D.C., to Cincinnati steam-powered streamliner the *Cincinnatian*. Four of the famed President class Pacific types were treated to a two-tone blue and chrome-trimmed shrouding. Although emulating the bullet-nosed profile of previous steam-engine camouflage attempts the result was an uncluttered form that left open the rods and wheelwork of a steam locomotive and yet integrated motive power with train, a flowing harmony at speed.

In one of its more static moments No. 5301 gulps down a tankful of water at the Deshler, Ohio, water plug while the hogger, anxious to be off on schedule, watches impatiently for a finish to the exchange of mail and express. The revenue density on the original routing never reached profit proportions; so the streamliner was transferred to a Cincinnati-Toledo run in 1950, where it rolled behind streamlined steam, in the face of ever-increasing dieselization, until late 1956. (*—Walter Peters*)

At right: Greatly removed from the impromptu shroud craze that is the subject of this section, the Pennsylvania's radical and impressive duplex-drive 4-4-4-4 T-1 class was both a streamlined steam locomotive and yet it was not. More an indicator of the trends in locomotive design to come — had not the diesel won out — than an attempt to capture the public fancy, the T-1 was intended as the long-awaited replacement for the K-4s Pacific on all east-west through passenger trains, regardless of equipment.

Little of the engine's 100-inch-diameter boiler was hidden beneath falsework, and whether the sharklike profile of the front end with its single Cyclopean eye was considered streamlining is a matter of conjecture.

In practical use the T-1 was a giant of a locomotive: fast, slippery on drivers when starting, smooth riding, dirty as a coal mine and impressive at speed or standing still. The locomotive lover lucky enough to be invited aboard for a ride in the cab would have a most thrilling experience.

It took nerve to stand up to a T-1 at full speed, for in that fast-approaching shark snout one could almost see the dreadful teeth, and to stand on an outside curve as that prow reeled off the tangent at a 100-plus an hour took more than just nerve — insane dedication to an obsession, one might call it. However, photographer Prusia stood his ground as T-1 No. 5517, with an unexplained dent in its pilot assembly, roared through a high-speed curve near Caseyville, Ill., with the westbound *Spirit of St. Louis* in the dreamers' days of 1946, when the T-1 was yet the promised savior of steam on the Pennsy. (*—both, C. E. Prusia*)

68

In glorious orange, red, black and silver, Southern Pacific's great GS-4 Northern No. 4444 poses regally for the photographer on a Los Angeles engine lead waiting to back down for the morning *Daylight* departure for San Francisco. Rare number combinations such as this were prime targets for the engine picture artists. (*—Robert J. Foster Collection*)

4. Engine Photographs

The photography of engines not in motion is both a lost art and one which seldom has received its due credit. The process of recording a favorite locomotive in the best possible light and pose was just that, an art. Granted that such views were the most recorded, outnumbering good action photographs by a hundred-to-one, the really beautiful locomotive still that we are concerned with here was not the rule but the exception. While the average photographer retained the orthodox view — early morning or late evening light to illuminate the undercarriage, rods on the bottom, clear and open background, and what came to be generally considered a three-quarter angle the better to show both side and front of the subject — the work of the best photographers encompassed a little something extra. They had to wait for a little better light, perhaps, and persist in having the locomotive moved to a more open location. Akin to the usual womanly plea to have the best side of her face photographed, they managed to pose each locomotive in a manner that would feature that particular design characteristic, be it the lordly browed look of an Elesco feedwater heater or the ready-for-the-charge feel of a pair of angular air-pump shields on the pilot deck. The results of this extra effort — and admittedly at times, pure luck — were portraits of the American steam locomotive that are cherished as highly by their owners as others would cherish an old master.

In the eyes of the still-desirous beholder of steam, the works of these people are indeed the works of masters. Without the efforts of these masters of the engine still in recording the age of steam, we would indeed be the poorer, for while all relish the action, the speed and the dramatics of a smoke-engulfed, on-the-move shot, it requires a really fine static pose to display the beauty of thin-spoked eighty-inch drivers, the plumber's nightmare of an Elesco feedwater system, the intricacies of a Baker valve gear and all the awe-inspiring mechanical mysteries that made the steam locomotive a thing of beauty in the eyes of its admirers.

It is then altogether fitting that a chapter in the history of contemporary steam railroad photography be set aside to commemorate the dedicated efforts of these masters, efforts that today comprise one of our most valued records of the steam locomotive's appearance. Many rail lovers engaged in this phase of photography, but here we are concerned only with the masters. While this narrows the field, the number of memorable shots remaining is still impossible to cover adequately in this single chapter. That is why the author has chosen one photographer to represent the masters; this should be done with an apology to others in the field, but truly no apology is needed, for everyone will agree that this photographer is a legend, an example of the fortitude, persistence and all-consuming desire that typified them all.

The late Robert J. Foster of East St. Louis, Illinois, was indeed a master. His persistent desire for quality and perfection earned for him the reputation of the dean of locomotive photographers. Even today, when a group of railroad buffs convene to discuss steam locomotives, his name eventually is mentioned, and invariably someone offers a pocketful of his now famous and prized postcard-sized locomotive prints. For the many individuals still imbued with a passion for the iron horse, these prints are the only link between the internal-combustion coldness of today and the once teeming days of the steam locomotive.

Like so many of his calling, Robert Foster desired to preserve each and every locomotive in existence, a noble achievement if it were possible. The remarkable thing, though, is that he came closer to accomplishing this feat than any other photographer. Undaunted by the constantly recurring obstacles of bad weather, distance, uncooperative railroad employees and sometimes just plain bad luck, he returned again and again to the same location to achieve just the right shot of just that particular locomotive. Overnight drives from home base were the rule, in order to take advantage of the treasured early morning light. Where distances were too great to allow his personal attention in photographing a certain locomotive, he established valuable relationships with others of like interest and coached them in the refinements of the art. His persistence was unending and knew no bounds; that this persistence paid off is evident in just the few of his memorable portraits pictured here.

Every locomotive was a face to him, and if its appearance were altered in any respect it must immediately be recorded again to show the difference. His knowledge of locomotive equipment rosters was phenomenal: he knew every engine, what it looked like, where it could be found and even what it sounded like. An evening spent with this gentleman, poring through his print library and listening to his experiences, was indeed a time to be relished. A part of the steam locomotive era ended in the early 1960s with the unfortunate passing of Mr. Foster and the subsequent dismantling of his large and valued collection of photographs.

The master's touch is here exhibited in a Foster rendering of Mobile and Ohio 4-6-2 No. 267 waiting to back into the East St. Louis, Ill., terminal for a morning southbound passenger haul. The engine crew, being quite familiar with the photographer's desires, have spotted the engine, rods down, in an area without obstructions and unappealing backdrops. These factors, plus the highly prized low morning angle of the sun, have helped create a masterpiece of locomotive photography.

One must give some credit to the subject itself, No. 267 being a true and unaltered product of the World War I United States Railroad Administration locomotive build-ing program that originated designs which remain second to none in the matter of symmetry, of shape, compactness and the well-balanced look.

Here at Argentine, Kans., the photographer has waited until there was enough smoke to create a hazy, indistinct-ness in the background structures, which might otherwise steal attention from the locomotive itself. In this case the smoke actually enhances the overall bigness and brute looks of Santa Fe Northern type No. 3766, just in from a predawn romp across the plains of Kansas. (—both, Robert J. Foster)

Hot and sweaty but beaming with the pride of self-accomplishment in having bagged one of his all time favorites (a New York Central Mohawk at Niles, Mich.), Robert J. Foster is pictured here as the very prototype of his calling nationwide. In contrast to the relatively minute and fast-firing cameras of today's steamless society, Mr. Foster clutches the more accepted and widely used photographic tools of his day: the heavily constructed wooden tripod for steadiness, atop of which is mounted the properly ordained and respected postcard Kodak, the recognized tool of the masters, without which no sane or serious-minded railroad photographer would have dared venture forth.

Mr. Foster's speed and agility with this cumbersome equipment was nothing short of amazing. His appearance meant only one thing to hostlers and their helpers in the engine yards he most often frequented: move the engine out in the open, rods on the sunny side on the bottom quadrant, the bell in a stilled position; cut off all steam leaks; and then stand back in the center of the cab while with computerlike precision he fires off six shots in rapid succession. In nearly every engine terminal in the Midwest his wishes exerted more influence than the commands of the company officials themselves.

74

Running extra and running fast, two Union Pacific speed queens, 4-8-2s Nos. 7019 and 7852 are giving 22 cars of midwestern farm boys a quick look at the desert scenery before they depart for heretofore unheard of waters and islands. (—*William K. Barham*)

5. Main Trains and Troop Sleepers

It is unfortunate that many future riders of rail passenger service received — or perhaps more correctly, suffered — their first experience at train riding on one of the many military specials of World War II. It was often their first and, if a choice later presented itself, last journey by rail. Comfort being one of the least concerns of the trip's sponsors, equipment was often gleaned from the boneyard, and the service was anything but extra-fare super de luxe. However, with everything on wheels pressed into service under the demands of moving men and matériel across the country, this laxity in comfort and service was not entirely of the carriers' making. With something like 43,700,000 troops, both men and women, on the move either in special cars coupled to regular schedules or on the 113,891 special military trains operated in the years 1941-45, along with the accompanying boom in civilian passenger traffic, it was a miracle that the nation's railroads, still climbing out of the depths of the Depression, could muster the equipment for such a Herculean job. Ironically, the Depression itself had fostered the need for the railroads to squeeze every ounce of effort out of every locomotive and more miles out of each piece of rolling stock.

Tourist sleepers, unused during the bleak years prior to Pearl Harbor and thoughtfully stored by the Pullman Company instead of being scrapped, became a mainstay of the many military specials. However, more reminiscent of the many main trains (synonym for the troop specials), and perhaps better remembered by their victims, were the box-shaped troop sleepers rushed through the shops of Pullman Standard and American Car and Foundry in a frantic effort to provide the needed rolling space for the military. Essentially a barracks on wheels with three layers of bunks and only the bare other necessities, neither of which could be settled upon with any degree of stability, they were no paradigm of comfort or luxury, but admittedly an improvement over the "40 et 8s" of World War I fame. (These were the French equivalent of the American boxcar whose militarily assigned capacity was forty men and eight mules.) The World War II troop sleepers were totally devoid of the amenities of soundproofing, air conditioning and smoothness of ride. Attempting to return from the diner to one's appointed accommodations while balancing a tray of already well-mixed army chow at 85 an hour behind a pair of raving Pennsy K-4s was a feat equal to the tightrope antics of Ringling Brothers' best.

Whole trains of combined troop sleepers and tourist Pullmans became commonplace, especially so on the single-track lines of the West where routings were less selective and distances great enough to warrant such assemblages. Main trains in every sense of the word, they held to the main line while passenger and freight runs alike took to the sidings to allow undisputed passage.

At the peak of the war effort, Cajon Pass in Southern California echoes to the drumbeats of the main trains in 1944, as illustrated here by the serious countenance of Santa Fe's big-tanked 2-10-2 No. 3901, approaching Summit with a solid 24-car mixed train of troop sleepers and tourist Pullmans running as third No. 3.
(*—William K. Barham*)

Swelling the dispatcher's train sheets, not to mention his headaches, the heavy wartime freight extras were packed in the sidings or straining at the yard limits to be out and moving on the main between the heavy flow of main trains and extra sections of the scheduled varnish hauls. Cajon Pass was a special headache, with the traffic flow of the two big western carriers, Santa Fe and Union Pacific, to be reckoned with on heavy grades. Both systems threw their mightiest muscles into the effort, with big-time steam power in multiples. In the U.P.'s case roaring Mallets such as 2-8-8-0 No. 3555, flying the white rags of an extra on its pilot beam, and Challenger No. 3829, laying down a cloud of oil smoke over the 100 assorted stock and refrigerator cars thundering behind, are double-headed on the upgrade out of Victorville, Calif., in 1944. (*—William K. Barham*)

Below, right Troop bunk cars and tourist Pullmans were a far cry from the luxurious air-conditioned lounges and sleeping cars of the *Grand Canyon Limited*, shown getting out of Vaughn, N.Mex., behind big-barreled Northern type No. 3781 and three units of Alco-built diesel power. At the time of this exposure, 1953, troop sleepers as such were a thing of the past, all having been scrapped or sold to various carriers for use as mail-storage cars or track-gang bunk cars.

Top, right Once upon a time . . . a wartime crowd with the military greatly in predominance awaits the opening of the train gates and the evening departures at the St. Louis Union Station in 1944. It was a far cry from the desolation now prevalent at this and other once teeming terminals. (*—Missouri Pacific Lines*)

6. *Smoky Citadels*

The steam locomotive is now gone from this land — as of this writing, gone some twelve to twenty years, depending upon what particular carrier one considers. In its passing it took with it a host of closely related and highly specialized facilities and appurtenances that existed only to serve the iron horse. Just as the Model T chugging around the village square, with the consequent elimination of the flesh-and blood horse, rendered obsolete the town watering trough; so too did the change in eating and resting habits of the diesel electric signal the retirement of the iron horse's stables, his feeding racks, watering troughs and even many of his caretakers.

The speed with which these changes were effected was no less surprising than that with which the seemingly irreplaceable steam locomotive itself was replaced. As systematically as man has attempted to render extinct the giant blue whale, the whooping crane, the American alligator and at times himself, he has undertaken the complete elimination of all traces of the iron horse. That he has succeeded in this case is unquestionable. Ironically, the dinosaurs that walked the earth some 75,000,000 years ago have left their fossilized imprints in a thousand discovered and yet undiscovered havens, yet in the mere decade since the iron horse ceased to trod our earth all traces of his existence have disappeared.

The smoky citadel, the smoky engine terminal where the iron horse came for rest and a meal has disappeared completely from the American scene. Once as important a part of the community as today's clover-leaf intersection, the engine-house and its related and readily identifiable structures dominated the horizon of many a rural community, if not with timber and concrete at least with towering columns of coal smoke that marked well the location for the steam searcher and were well remarked by the housewife with a fresh wash hung out to dry.

The most distinguishable and peculiar structure in the engine terminal group was the wholly steam-oriented roundhouse itself. Always encircling the essential turntable pit, the building was variously large or small, depending on the importance of the terminal, but always in the semicircular or the near full-circle shape. Some of the larger roundhouses, such as the Norfolk and Western's at Roanoke or the Pennsylvania's at Altoona, burgeoned into fully complete circles, and double ones at that!

A roundhouse interior as viewed from the outside was always dark and forbidding, a feeling heightened as the headlights of parked locomotives peering out through the usually large and dirty windows at tracks' end took on the appearance of the single great eye of a Cyclopean monster that followed one without blinking. For the sidelines admirer of the steam locomotive to gather courage and enter within the premises of the giant's own resting place could be likened unto the first step of the knight errant into Grendel's lair. A modern steam locomotive was a big machine, looming even larger within the confines of this building, posing solemn and majestic, commanding the awe-struck admirer to divide his thoughts between admiration and, if official permission had not been available for the visit, fear that at any moment he would be thrust out into the sunlight before traveling the full circle of rapture.

The foregoing paragraph will surely bring forth a snort of derision from those who labored daily within these engine stalls, which were of course only a place for servicing and making minor repairs to the iron horse. The enginehouse was a place of continuous toil, and hardly does one's place of labor bring forth a feeling of awe. For the lover of steam, though, it was a Mecca to the faithful and, like Mecca, not given to being adequately photographed, inside or out. Photographic records of the once plentiful enginehouses across the continent are few, an unfortunate circumstance that applies to nearly all the structures and facilities related to the iron horse, such as the towering coal docks, water plugs and even the rural frame railroad depot, once the most important building in town.

With the advent of the diesel a whole new method of servicing and fueling was needed, and the steam-oriented facilities just didn't fill the bill. The grimy old enginehouses were either razed entirely or sold to private firms doing a variety of businesses. The turntable pits have filled in and become automobile parking lots, part of a once creeping, now galloping mania to cover the earth with sterile asphalt.

The domineering coaling docks that stood guard over most engine terminals seemed to withstand the destruction a little while longer than their contemporaries, due principally to nothing more than sheer strength, especially in the case of concrete structures. Only with the aid of explosives and that scourge of mother earth, the bulldozer, were they too finally removed from the scene. Lamentably the rail photographer's attention was too often focused only on the locomotive taking on fuel, and the structure itself was given little attention. Coaling facilities came in all shapes and sizes, as custom-built as the steam engine itself. They were variously of timber, concrete and in the case of the later Fairbanks styles, all metal; with few exceptions most straddled the servicing tracks, allowing gravity to propel the coal toward the waiting tender bunkers.

It is indeed unfortunate that more of the locomotive servicing operations are not preserved on film. The grimy, smoky confines of most engine terminals were, to be quite honest, dirty and perhaps a bit dangerous to the inexperienced, but their very atmosphere lent mystery to the steam machine itself, much as fire and brimstone would befit the appearance of the devil.

The photographic achievements to date that do exist were arduously won with great patience and cost to the nervous system, in locations where actual hindrance to the honest airs of the steam admirer was encountered, a hindrance mostly attributable to the idiot urgencies which motivate the general intelligence in time of war — this latter event having become a rather continuous affair — that in turn became a rather overdone excuse for prohibiting the photographing of service facilities. Away from the busy and oftentimes restricted engine leads of the terminals, out on the main at a distance calculated to correspond with designated tender capacities, the towering coaling structures were a special haven for the quick-thinking photographer. The need for fuel and water brought the swift-moving trains to an impatient halt at these earlier-style pit stops, offering the steam admirer an unhindered opportunity to see, hear and photograph routine activities similar to those of the engine terminal.

The sounds of locomotive servicing have largely been ignored in our records of steam. As the whistle in the night is held synonymous with the iron horse, so too, should be the sound of black diamonds cascading down the metal pans and into the tender bunkers with a dull thud, the clank of the water hatch as the fireboy slams it shut on the tender top, the "oohkay" sung out to the hogger, signifying a slow move ahead so that the bunker can be evenly piled with coal — all this intermingled with the secure thump of the air compressors or the whine of a generator, terminating in a crescendo of wide-open stack thunder as the iron pony, his belly full, lumbers into motion on sanded rails.

The shape of the citadel, basically circular with all tracks radiating from the center of the turntable, is graphically demonstrated in this overhead view of the Missouri Pacific's relatively large facility that once existed at St. Louis. Typical of hundreds of such installations across the land, all the basic ingredients are included here: the circular enginehouse, turntable and pit, in and outbound servicing tracks, outside storage stall tracks and accompanying facilities. As with nearly all such onetime havens of steam power, the same air view today would show only the sterile asphalt of a parking lot for automobiles. (—*Wayne Leeman Collection*)

A quick-thinking company photographer of the onetime New York Central System recorded not only both sides of Niagara No. 6000 as it rode the table but also the entire layout of the famed engine terminal at Harmon, N.Y., in all-steam days (or so it would appear from the lack of internal combustion power in the views). The distant coal dock, inbound and outbound engine servicing leads, the powerhouse and the smoke-encrusted enginehouse are all visible in this sweeping panorama. Steam purists of the "Central," as would those of any allegiance, will strain their eyes to see what engines are in the darkened stalls. (*—New York Central System*)

Below The outside stalls of the Cincinnati Union Terminal always sported a wide variety of passenger power at rest. Various orthodox and stream-styled power of the C.&O., Pennsy and N.&W. are on display this September day of 1947. (*—Charles Kerrigan*)

Below In the more temperate climates of the South and Southwest open-air enginehouses were the vogue. While Pacific type No. 367 takes a spin on the table, Mikado No. 914 rests inside the Missouri-Kansas-Texas' open-sided two-staller at Denison, Tex., altogether a fitting structure for the always-conservative Katy Lines. (*—R. S. Plummer*)

A bird's-eye view of Class H 4-8-4 No. 3013 is afforded from the coal dock at Proviso, where just in from Omaha it waits a turn for ash removal and a rubdown.

Top right One of the largest, and a close contender for the grimiest, enginehouses was the Chicago and North Western's at the famed freight terminal of Proviso at Chicago, Ill. At the height of its use during World War II the turntable was almost never without engine weight upon it. Mikado No. 2493 eases off the table to pull a cold-boilered sister out of the house to the fuel tracks. (*—both, C.&N.W. Railroad*)

The steam locomotive encountered in its lair at night was a mysterious beast emitting almost frightening sounds and flashes of light. The sense of hearing comes up to par with sight during the hours of darkness, and every sigh, creak or groan added to an atmosphere already charged with intrigue and fascination.

Adding to the din, Illinois Central 0-8-0 No. 3530 reposes on the table in the center of the Centralia, Ill., roundhouse with safety valves popping and blower roaring, building up a head of steam for the night's yard chores. (—*Richard Wallin*)

Not every engine terminal was generously endowed with enginehouses, coal chutes or motive power as big as the Union Pacific's at North Platte, Nebr., pictured here with every lead track occupied by some of the world's largest locomotives. (—Kenneth McDonald Collection)

The complete opposite would be the Dardenelle and Russellville's tidy little terminal in the Arkansas metropolis for which the "D" stands. Its entire engine terminal stands nakedly exposed in this singular view, not to mention 100% of its motive power and nearly 50% of its employees. Ten-

Wheeler No. 11 rests half in, half out of the open-stall enginehouse, while offices in an ancient grounded combine, a shed for tools, a water tank and a coal dock of less than skyscraper proportions complete the facilities. Coaling up is performed by dropping the tilted chute into the tender bunker and having a couple of locally hired laborers alternately toss shovels of the black stuff into the chute. Cinder removal, a job of major proportions in large terminals, is also efficiently dealt with by means of a No. 10 scoop, a wheelbarrow and time taken out from the paper work to clean up the day's droppings. (—Johnnie Gray)

A complete facility and a ready customer are both evident in this singular exposure: steel coal dock, water tank, sand tower, water and oil cranes; and over the ash pit is a U.S.R.A. heavy Mikado of the Colorado and Southern at Denver. (—*Milt Nafus*)

"Run for the roundhouse, Nellie, he can't corner you there" — a backwoodsy admonition to the town beauty fleeing from an overzealous suitor — would have little value if this structure were her only recourse. This minute ancestor of multiple-stalled facilities to come was located at Thayer, Mo., on the Frisco Railroad. (—*Wayne Leeman Collection*)

Thump, thump, thump, thump — and all eight drivers of Mikado No. 1435 drop off the table tracks of the Dupo, Ill., enginehouse. The hostler's helper riding the pilot steps gives a slow come ahead sign as the big-boilered freight engine, all oiled, greased and inspected in the house, is moved down to the outbound lead to await the arrival of the road crew. (—*Missouri Pacific*)

The turntable was the focal point of all operations in the engine terminal; no locomotive could enter or leave the enginehouse without its use. The front and rear of a steam locomotive being very different things, the turning of a locomotive became of prime importance.

The first turntable known to have been used in the United States was on the Granite Railway, a small line opened in October of 1826 to carry blocks of granite from the Bunker Hill quarry in Quincy, Mass., to a wharf on the Neponset River, 2¾ miles away. The granite was floated to Boston and used to erect a monument at the site of the Battle of Bunker Hill; the monument still stands but the railroad and its archetypal turntable have long been abandoned. Cars of the Granite Railway were drawn by horses and it was the cars that were turned, the locomotive having yet to make its appearance. Thus we had a turntable before we had a locomotive.

Rock Island R-67 class 4-8-4 No. 5114 is about to take a circular ride on the Silvis, Ill., table, which apparently has no protective shanty for operator or controls, unusual in a climate where cold and ice could hamper both. (*—Charles Kerrigan*)

Burlington's beloved Mikado No. 4960 is swung into position for another of her famous railfan trips in the early 1960s out of St. Louis. The Q's turntable at this location is of the through-truss type construction, a style favored by the road and its subsidiaries.

By the very nature of their age most roundhouses were becoming rather decrepit, in the last years of steam, obviously attributable to the operating departments' growing allegiance to the newer internal-combustion power. Even in the glory days of steam, however, most enginehouses were dark and forbidding places, especially at night, when a single bulb and reflector supplied the only illumination.

Management's infatuation and eventual wedlock with the diesel electric changed this environment drastically; in short, nothing was too good for the newcomer. Towering brick-and-steel structures, generously skylighted; sunken inspection pits for the running gear, amply illuminated by bays of fluorescent tubes; electric-powered gantry cranes replacing the muscle and sweat of the grime-coated roundhouse machinist — all these modern-day improvements became commonplace on the railroad scene. A virtual revolution in the servicing of motive power has transpired.

Consider the giant and, in 1949, new diesel facility of the Rock Island at Silvis, Ill. Shafts of sunlight reach into every corner and, where hindered in passage, are replaced by a multitude of fluorescent tubes. (*—Charles Kerrigan*)

On the other hand, inside the Baltimore and Ohio's aging house at Lorain, Ohio, a 2-8-2 and a 2-8-8-4 seek the warmth of a single incandescent bulb. (*—Walter Peters*)

A trio of dirty-faced little urchins, an 0-6-0 and a pair of 2-8-0s, sit staring across the turntable pit of the Pennsylvania's Louisville, Ky., enginehouse at K-4s Pacific No. 1329 which, contrary to its grimy exterior, is serviced and ready to depart with a late evening passenger run to Indianapolis.

One of the hazards awaiting the itinerant and inexperienced rail photographer was between the rails, a waist-deep ash pit like that seen on the nearest track. Quite often kept full of water to cool the red-hot ash upon dumping, the resultant mixture took on the appearance of solid ground. Well etched in the author's memory is the fleeting picture of a fellow photographer, bent upon yet a little more perspective through his camera finder, who stepped backward into one of these caldrons of grit and ash, thereupon sinking chest-deep into the muck. Though having the soundness of mind to hold his camera high above his head, his activities for the day were greatly curtailed. (—*Jack Fravert*)

97

Ever wonder how those especially designed and sophisticated company identification markings get on the side of locomotives and tender? A steady hand and a practical eye do it, in this case to a Baltimore and Ohio 4-8-2 tender in the Willard, Ohio, enginehouse. (—*Walter Peters*)

Ready, aim, fire! A battery of camera-wielding railfans line up to record Union Pacific's No. 844 being attended to on a 1961 Cheyenne-Rawlins, Wyo., excursion run. The famous big Northern type is receiving plenty of attention at this Laramie station stop, reminiscent of many a not-too-distant steam-powered limited making the required ten-minute inspection stop. The blue flag is hung on the cab front, grease guns ram their loads around the main pins, and on the tender deck both fuel oil and water are being taken on in quantities generous enough to fill the ravenous gullet of that centipede tender.

he inbound lead tracks keep filling up ith trains that have run all night, and will be hours before the hostler's crew s them all serviced, fueled and put to st in the Illinois Central's East St. ouis, Ill., enginehouse. (—*Walter Peters*)

he admonition to "save water" was a current one in all engine terminals, apearing both on the bulletin boards and employee instructions. After all, the quid stuff was needed in great quanties and it did cost money, in pure and eated form alike. The warning is espeally appropriate in the photo at left as e hostler reaches frantically with his ook to staunch the Niagaralike cascade er the side of a big Missouri Pacific nder that has been filled to capacity d then some! (—*Robert J. Foster*)

Bestial in their manners, a pair of New York Central Alco hood units jut forth from the old brick enginehouse at White Plains, N.Y., now possessed of these black-and-gray growlers, and dare an old-time resident to again enter therein. Little should be their annoyance, though, for Pacific No. 4549 is making one of its last swings on the table in the closing days of steam-powered commuter runs in and around Gotham City. (—New York Central)

Below, amid the smoky confusion of the joint New York Central-Chesapeake and Ohio engine terminal at Louisville, Ky., an 0-8-0 of the likewise jointly owned Louisville and Jefferson Bridge and Belt Railroad pauses in its efforts to wye the cars of the recently arrived George Washington of the C.&O. In the background is the J class 4-8-2 that just brought in the string of streamlined, heavyweight varnish. (—Jack Fravert)

Gothenburg, Nebr., has heard its share of stack exhausts as many a big-boilered Northern or Challenger has barked away from the fueling dock there, its progress across the high-speed Nebraska division having been slowed by a need for fuel and water.

The lead 2-10-2 on a westbound double-header has filled its bunkers and now fumes impatiently while its twin gets a share. The U.P. had a great number of coal docks of steel and iron construction, perhaps more than any other railroad, the general preference elsewhere being timber or concrete. (—*Charles Kerrigan*)

A trio of Baltimore and Ohio 4-8-2s, at right, face off in the shadow of the Garrett, Ind., coal dock. (—*Walter Peters*)

Washing trains was no task for a Monday-morning wash maid. To cut the grease and accumulated road grime took a lot of high-pressure steam mixed with kerosene and applied with great force. In the great days of steam every locomotive arriving at the engine terminal was given a bath as a routine matter; in later years the operating department's inclination to continue the practice diminished almost entirely. Latter day steam enthusiasts thus find it hard to visualize a Pennsy K-4s with brightly polished boiler flanks, graphite smokeboxes and red cab roofs, all of which were commonplace before.

Passenger-hauling 4-8-2 No. 414 of the Louisville and Nashville receives a scrubbing at the South Louisville, Ky., enginehouse before being allowed inside for servicing. (—*Jack Fravert*)

At right an Illinois Central 2-8-2 has its feet scrubbed. (—*Elmer Onstott*)

Washday Monday was every day here. (—*Missouri Pacific Lines*)

Even apple green gets grimy climbing those Carolina hills. Southern's PS-4 No. 1372 takes a bath at Spartanburg, S.C. (—*Gordon Sherman*)

The sight of a photographer in this isolated area of Curtis Hill was certain to bring instant attention from the head-end crew, and the fireman on Prairie No. 1805 is no exception as he stares back in disbelief upon discovering a camera lens zeroed in on him and his charge. (*—Preston George*)

7. *Curtis Hill, Courtesy Preston George*

While most of the nation's geographic areas could boast of both known and unknown photographers recording the railroading peculiar to that region, the windswept, barren rails of Oklahoma could count their followers at most on the fingers of one hand. Chief among these loyal followers was one who traipsed to the far corners of the finger-pointing state in search of the far-flung and oftentimes far-between railroading. Preston George had to be loyal and sometimes stubborn to ferret out the best that Oklahoma had to offer, and Curtis Hill on the Santa Fe's southern district in the far northwest corner of the state was one of those finds made only through stubborn persistence.

Associated with memories of Santa Fe operations are visions of double-shotted freights and varnish hauls making accelerated runs for the towering mountain passes of Cajon and Raton in the rugged setting of California and Colorado. Quite the opposite held true with little-known and seldom photographed Curtis Hill: located in a region far from any great concentrations of population and definitely not regarded as a candidate for travel-poster material. However, the grade possessed an element of rugged desolation and intriguing operations that lured Preston George to cover it by photograph, literally foot by foot, and we are the richer for his work.

Hampered by 1944 wartime gas rationing but feeling an urgency occasioned by a program of line relocation that the Santa Fe had just undertaken to ease the restrictive curves encountered throughout the climb, Preston George had just discovered the photographic possibilities of the grade, and he made a determined effort to record its operations in fair weather or foul before it was too late. Automobile trips that started well before dawn and covered many miles of unimproved dirt roads were part of his schedule, and on location a dawn-to-dusk vigil was the rule.

Once out of the division point at Waynoka, on the western edge of the high flat Enid Prairies, the single-track iron winds and snakes its way tortuously around and through one dry wash and arroyo after another before the summit of a ridge that separates the waters of the Cimarron and Canadian rivers is reached. Abounding in tight flange-squealing curves, the grade was a thorn in the side of operations men who were accustomed to "rolling 'em" on the flat, straight right of way in adjacent Kansas and Texas. The rail straightening that occurred as Preston continued his coverage was a natural move for the Santa Fe, and while something of the rugged look was eliminated in the process, the wide gentle curves that resulted were a thing of beauty.

The most distinctive feature of Curtis Hill operations was the helper locomotives. While the Santa Fe employed machines of noble proportions and generous wheel arrangements on other distant mountain-climbing operations, the motive power department allocated this task at Curtis Hill to a group of fifty-year-old machines of the 2-6-2 wheel arrangement, ironically termed "Prairie types" for the terrain over which they were originally created to operate most efficiently. While most of their kind ended up in service on the innumerable branch lines of their respective systems, here on Curtis Hill they were the main helper power. What more incongruous sight could exist than to watch as a brawny, monstrous 4-8-4 or 2-10-4, the world's largest at that, would thunder by and a hundred cars later a compact and prim little Prairie type would bring up the rear. Belying appearances, however, the classic design pulled — or rather, pushed — its share of the load.

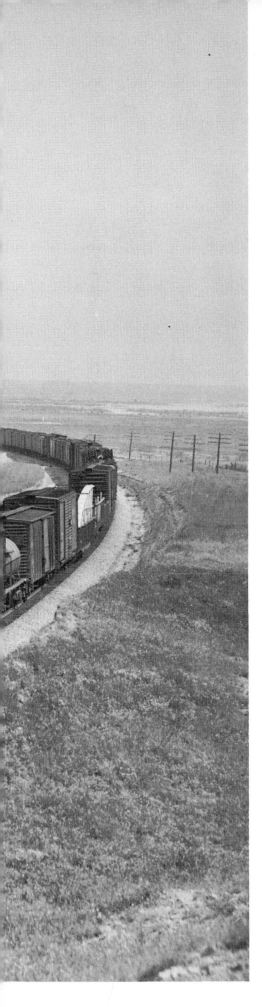

Coming and going on Curtis Hill. One of the Santa Fe's finest, 4-8-4 No. 2903, is getting a run on the hill at Belva, Okla., with 85 cars while Prairie type No. 1806 churns up the tail wind. The helper sports a 12-wheel tender of odd design that is a remnant from the Santa Fe's short-lived venture into Mallet articulated power. (*—Preston George*)

Big-boned 2-10-4 No. 5302 rolls effortlessly downgrade at close to sixty an hour with a 100-car reefer block stretching behind on the newly laid curve at Belva, Oklahoma. The old line lay in the shadow of the barren bluff in the distance. (*—Preston George*)

No. 1886, a dapper dan in the Santa Fe roster, does its stuff at the rear of a westbound string of empties on the grade; a robust Texas type is 105 cars ahead. (—*Preston George*)

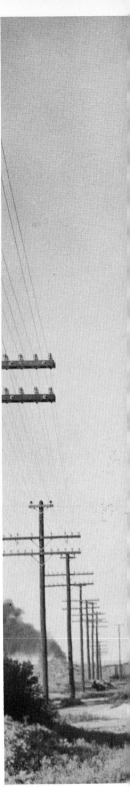

Hot spot at the top in a quiet moment. Although not a train is in sight, it is still hot in the noon sun of an Oklahoma summer at Curtis Depot, the summit of its namesake grade. A typical prairie train-order office it is, with passing track, water plug and complete isolation, except for the ribbons of steel. Quiet one moment, teeming with activity the next. Centralized traffic control finally eliminated Curtis Station, as it did countless other such prairie oases, and the western prairie is drearier for the lack of them. (—*Preston George*)

One of the earlier series of brawny Santa Fe 2-10-4s, No. 5003 comes storming through Quinlan, halfway up Curtis Hill, with a westbound extra. Ninety cars behind the huge box-shaped tender can be seen the smoke of dapper dan Prairie type No. 1886, putting in its last days of service in this 1947 scene. (—*Preston George*)

Substituting for the usual Prairie type helper, a double-domed Mikado adds its muscle to that of Santa Fe No. 3902 in hoisting 102 mixed loads and empties at Belva, Okla. (*—Preston George*)

Before the Santa Fe relocated the line over Curtis Hill, the world's largest 4-8-4, No. 2901, is seen here negotiating the tight curves of the old grade in 1945, with the 15 heavyweight cars of second No. 23, the *Grand Canyon*, and looking completely out of place for all its efforts on the rain-slick rails. (—*Preston George*)

Through mail and express extras, such as Hudson type No. 3455 is here seen wheeling west of Olathe, Kans., went via the Santa Fe's southern district and Curtis Hill but largely ignored a helping hand and made the summit unassisted.

Back Bay — or more explicitly South Bay Junction — Boston, is the scene of New Haven freight BN-3 banging through a maze of crossovers behind beetle-browed Mountain type No. 3501, obviously suffering from an acute case of defective cylinder packing. (*—Wayne Brumbaugh*)

8. *Rarely Seen Eastern Scenes*

Big roads and little, short lines and main lines, all these in abundance once laced the heavily populated and industrialized northeastern United States, making a paradise of railroad activity with unmatched variety. Appropriately therefore, the area could also boast the highest density of railfans and photographers, who almost daily recorded the unending thunder on the mighty New York Central's four-track main along the Hudson, or the cliff-hanging action on the Pennsylvania's Horseshoe Curve, not to mention the incessant hum of the GG-1s on the Jersey meadows. With all this pulse-quickening action on the multiple mains over which the rail barons of yesteryear fought, there remained a score of carriers not quite so immense but which, when discovered in the right location, could put on a show equal to or even better than their headline-hugging brethren.

It is small wonder then that, as with many smaller first-class systems, there were rail buffs whose first love and loyalty was to these less publicized operations and their not-so-familiar equipment, rather than to the loudly lauded and relatively over-publicized four-track systems. It is fortunate, indeed, that such was the loyalty of some photographers, for we would be the poorer without a photographic record of such eastern gems as the Lackawanna and the Lehigh Valley, both of which operated more aesthetic varieties of the 4-8-4 wheel arrangement than any other railroad system; or the Delaware and Hudson, whose hunchbacked and heavy Consolidations of Loree legend vied with multiples of polished, high-wheeled Challenger types pulling and pushing the loads of anthracite out of the black holes of Pennsylvania. In the midst of all this the Lehigh and Hudson River did a thriving bridge-traffic business behind what must surely have been the most impressively heavy looking 2-8-0s to crush the ballast of any road, while not far away the Erie operated the largest fleet of Berkshire types in existence, and good-looking ones to boot! Somewhat closer to the Canadian woods, in down-East country the Central Vermont defied local allegiance and operated the only Texas types in a land where motive power of more moderate size was the accepted thing.

Wander through these rarely viewed scenes of big eastern railroading off the beaten path, as recorded by the cameras of Robert Collins and Wayne Brumbaugh, whose coverage of these roads in the days of steam is one of the most extensive in existence. Both of these gentlemen are rarities in the rail photographer's world, typified by the postman who enjoys a walk on his day off, since when not roaming the wooded valleys of Pennsylvania or New York both spend their professional hours dutifully dispatching the traffic of the Erie and the New Haven, respectively.

Road of contrasts was the Delaware and Hudson — combined coal hauler and bridge route; great experimenter in highly efficient but absurdly slow compound 2-8-0s and 4-8-0s; a carrier running English-styled motive power with capped stacks, elephant-ear smoke deflectors and the stern, unembellished lines generally distasteful to students of American steam power. Yet one has to admit that, out of all that was disliked in D.&H. steam power, when some of the more objectionable features were eliminated in 1940, with the help of American Locomotive Company draftsmen, the result was one of the more beautiful articulated locomotives. Literally a rebirth of steam as far as locomotive design on the carrier was concerned, these classic 4-6-6-4s, all 34 of them, were a drastic contrast to the center-cab

118

camelbacks, sluggish compound Mallets and beefy Consolidations whose fireboxes were in the last stages of gestation. An example of the latter is No. 1206, left, wheeling an incredible 102 cars south at Unadilla, N.Y., in 1941.

Well deserving of compliments yet ignoring them all, Challenger No. 1521 belches smoke like a true steam locomotive as it thunders between the arches of the storied Starruca viaduct at Lanesboro, Pa., with 99-car symbol freight RW-6.

Lithe of limb and graceful either in motion or at rest, touches of the unorthodox were apparent in recessed headlight, ever present D.&H. capped stack, recessed and illuminated headlight numbers and clean, uncluttered lines. *(—Robert Collins)*

Photographer Collins admits to having been lulled into a state of inattention by the postcardlike surroundings near Rockdale, Pa., before he was awakened by T-2-A Northern No. 5201 rocketing around the distant curve with 102 empties for coal loading further west. Regardless of the consist, be it time freight or empty hoppers, Lehigh Valley hoggers liked to rock 'n roll 'em.

Below More commonly dispatched behind a torpedo-nosed, red-and-black stream-styled Pacific of Otto Kuhler's devising, the New York-bound *John Wilkes* with refurbished standard equipment hits an even 75 over the knife-edged ballast near Bloomsburg, N.J., in 1942 behind the conventional-looking No. 2095. (*—both, Robert Collins*)

The author admits, with a sense of sadness and some guilt, to having experienced little or no exposure, either physically or photographically, to many of the carriers and locomotives described in this section, save one, the Lehigh Valley. A long-time favorite from afar, comparable with a closer-to-home favorite, the Wabash, the Lehigh Valley operated a fleet of aged Pacifics and more modern 4-8-2s and 4-8-4s on high-speed schedules over well-maintained roadbeds, just as did the Wabash.

Therefore, whenever the exigencies of military life would allow ample opportunity, such as during an enforced stay at an eastern base in the mid-1940s, a trip to Bound Brook, N.J., was the order of the day, there to witness and marvel at this Wabash of the East. The impressions left from those

visits are still with the author today: well-manicured roadbed and high speeds, oh, those high speeds with which a marvelous assortment of locomotives — at once both antique with their high-arched cab windows and modern with their drop-coupler pilots and all-welded tenders — roared to and fro in recurring spectacles of swirling drivers and hammering wheels.

The Lehigh Valley's main line from New York to Buffalo is a thing of beauty in double track and knife-edged ballasting; its iron traverses such tongue-twisting rustic hamlets as Meshappen, Mehoopany and Hokendauqua. T-2-B Northern No. 5218 is working steam, and smoke, through Wyalusing on the Susquehanna River with westbound time freight in 1947. (—H. D. Runey)

121

Where the action is, or was. Starruca, Pa., on October 14, 1951, was the arena for this spectacle of D.&H.'s finest, and photographer Collins was the sole spectator, as is often the case, to 36 white-rimmed drivers clawing over sanded rail on an obvious upgrade with the 120 loads and empties of RW-4. (—*Robert Collins*)

The 2-10-4 Texas type meant superpower, at least to other carriers employing this lengthened version of Lima's A-1 2-8-4. For the Central Vermont, however, it meant more axles to spread engine weight with, rather than high horsepower. Regardless of 60-inch drivers and 35 mile an hour speed restrictions, this biggest of all steam power in New England was an impressive-looking locomotive and performed well for the C.V., especially when bucking those also impressive New England snows. On a road where 2-8-0s and 4-6-0s were the rule, Texas No. 700 was quite a sight thundering through White River Junction, Vt., with time freight No. 430. (—Robert Collins)

A pair of Baltimore and Ohio E-60 class Consolidations are having a rough go of it moving a southbound freight up Newfield Hill on the line between Wellsville, N.Y., and Galeton, Pa., in 1955.

This trackage and the locomotives on it were part of the Buffalo and Susquehanna Railroad, which was acquired by the B.&O. in 1932 and at that time extended southwestward to a connection with the new owner's main line at Du Bois, Pa. A rather ironic and unusual situation resulted from a disastrous flood in 1942, when the portion of the line between Sinnamahoning and Burrows, Pa., was washed out so badly that the management decided not to rebuild but instead left the remaining V-shaped routes from Burrows and Galeton, Pa., to Wellsville and Addison, N.Y., isolated from the rest of the parent system. And

thus the two branches operated, physically cut off from the remainder of the system, until they were sold to the Wellsville, Addison and Galeton Railroad in 1955.

Six B.&O. ex-Buffalo and Susquehanna 2-8-0s, including the pair laboring here, were included in the sale, but the new owners elected to use diesel power instead, gradually selling off the Consolidations to raise funds for the internal-combustion units. Dieselization began with several 500-horsepower Whitcomb units; these were replaced in turn by some G.M. 120-ton units originally used by the Ford Motor Company, and as of this writing these outmoded machines have been replaced with three ex-Southern Pacific gray-and-red "bloody nose" FP-7 E.-M.D. units. (—Wayne Brumbaugh)

At left a tandem of Poconos, as the Lackawanna dubbed its 4-8-4 types, gets a roll on westbound tonnage at Clifton, N.J. The D.L.&W. pioneered in the dual-service wheel arrangement, introducing a 77-inch drivered machine for passenger service as early as 1927.

Were it not for the inward-sloping sand dome, a peculiarity of design that happily intrigued only the Lackawanna, No. 1631 in the lead of this double-header would rate top honors in a motive-power beauty contest. With a well-proportioned boiler, boxpok drivers and a tender of squarish design on six-wheel trucks (and ignoring the latter day "Mars" light addition), the facial features of this locomotive show extraordinarily good taste.

At left below "Miss Snow alights, her dress still white, she took the road of anthracite." The imaginary heroine of the Lackawanna's early publicity efforts would credit the air conditioning prominent on the last three cars of the Delaware, Lackawanna and Western's No. 2, the *Pocono Express,* following closely under a swirling black cloud put out by Pocono No. 1501, nearing the end of the eastward run at Roseville, N.J., in 1941.

A little giant of a railroad in steam days was the Lehigh and Hudson River, whose fat-boilered, Wooten-firebox-equipped 2-8-0s trundled incredibly heavy drags through such halcyon hamlets as Cranberry Lake, Allamuchy and Tranquility on the 86 miles of heavy-duty iron, a bypass around New York rail congestion for New England-bound freight.

It took persistence, and much stomping of the feet, to wait in the freezing cold for shots such as this, but the Vesuvian outpouring of smoke and steam well justifies the self-torture. Underneath it all is L.&H.R. big Consolidation No. 93, straining hard to urge 600 cold journals into motion at Hampton-burg, N.Y., circa 1941. (—all, Robert Collins)

Only five years apart in birth, yet altogether lacking in family resemblance, a pair of New York, Ontario and Western 4-8-2s pull and push a 95-car extra freight on the upgrade through Stony Ford, N.Y. While the pusher, No. 401, resplendent in a fresh coat of paint, has all the attributes of the home-office drafting board in its design, the lead engine could almost pass for a castoff L-2c Mohawk of the New York Central.

Judging from the neatly kept double-track iron, the well-shopped look of No. 401, the length of the train itself and the furor of activity in getting it over the system, things bode well for the N.Y.,O.&W. in 1942. Ill times would befall the road in post-World War II days, with its eventual demise in 1957, a tragedy that even the promised salvation of dieselization failed to stave off. (—Robert Collins)

Passenger revenues on the "Old and Weary" were always of a seasonal nature. Summer holidays and week ends filled the old and venerable equipment to bursting with Manhattanites fleeing the hot cement canyons for the cool quiet of the upstate New York lake country. The long winter months were another story, however, with the *Mountaineer* and *Ontario Express* running nearly vacant in the frigid blizzards.

A typical holiday special of the summer season — appropriately enough named the *Half Holiday* — filled with tired New Yorkers hustles through Fair Oaks, N.Y., on a Sunday evening in 1940 behind a bucking, swaying camelback Mogul of antiquated ancestry. (—*Robert Collins*)

At historic Faneuil, Mass., where seethed and flared the flames of the American Revolution in 1770, the flames and heat of a revolution in steam motive power can be seen as an original Lima superpower Berkshire of the Boston and Albany charges westward with freight destined for Albany and beyond.

The close clearances on most eastern carriers, notably the New York Central and its subsidiaries such as the B.&A. here, dictated definite limits for boiler diameter and cylinder width, but motive power deisgners retaliated by mounting every conceivable appliance and contrivance outside the boiler shell proper, resulting in a machine of formidable appearance. (—*Wayne Brumbaugh*)

Above Inseparably linked with the Berkshire legend were both the Nickel Plate and the Erie, the former perhaps more so because its own S class engines lived long into the sparse years of steam, when supply and demand played a key role in publicity. The Erie's S class 2-8-4s, although numerically superior (105 units versus the 80 on the Nickel Plate), were reined in some seven years before the Nickel Plate's machines. Garnering less publicity as a result of this earlier demise, Erie's machines benefited from the road's onetime six-foot gauge and resultant clearances by coming on big — big enough to compare favorably with the generous dimensions of western steam power. Over 16 feet at top of stack, with a boiler girth of 9 feet, the big S's made light of appliances that bulked large on most eastern power.

S-3 No. 3374 shows the why of it all, storming through Stony Ford, N.Y., with 86 cars of Buffalo-bound tonnage. (*—Robert Collins*)

Notwithstanding the boldface type in the *Official Guide*, announcing Monson Junction's location on the Bangor and Aroostook Railroad some 70 miles west of Bangor, Me., this scene of rustic tranquility reveals the complexities involved in running a rural junction in down-East Yankeedom.

With the branch to Monson proper, some two miles distant, veering to the right, the combined depot and agent's living quarters of generous dimensions, well-fortified against the New England winters, are the actual fixed properties. Individuals of importance are the owner and operator of the local feed store, down to meet the daily mixed easing all-too-quietly up to the depot platform behind a clanking Ten-Wheeler. Its consist includes a combination coach-baggage of archaic ancestry and a sway-backed boxcar from which the feed lot operators and the train crew will wrestle a score of loaded feed sacks. This is the high point of the day's activities, barring Sunday of course, at Monson Jct. (*—Wayne Brumbaugh*)

left On a cold February morning one can hear the ...es crack in the intense and quiet cold. Cracking even ...re loudly and glistening in the reflected light of the ...w-covered right of way, Erie 4-6-2 No. 2533 bounds ...o view with a Gotham-bound local at Waldwick, N.J., ...1940. (*—Robert Collins*)

All the excitement and drama of mountain railroading is condensed in this Kindig rendering of two compound Mallets clawing at the rails and tearing at the skies as they rage through Pinecliff, Colo., on the 2% ascending to Moffat Tunnel with the *Ute* on June 25, 1939. Despite the clamour and towering plume of smoke the pace is a steady 15 miles an hour with little opportunity for an increase immediately ahead.

Probably best known for his coverage of both standard and narrow-gauge lines of the Denver and Rio Grande Western, although his reputation with the Union Pacific's Sherman Hill ranks a close second, Mr. Kindig's artistry has been exhibited greatly over the years in various railroad publications. However, he comments that lately requests for his work are less frequent, an unfortunate sign of the times in an increasingly diesel-oriented fraternity, assuredly a significant loss to both the historian and the still-smitten lover of steam. (*—Richard Kindig*)

9. Because They Were There: Mountain Climbers in Steam and Soul

Much has been written about the mountain men who braved the heights of the western mountain wilderness in search of riches, and about the hell-roaring camps they created and peopled in the high places of the Rockies, where souls of lesser stuff were sent scurrying by the monumental elements. The history of Western America is resplendent with the adventures not only of the determined and the dreamers who sought out the riches under the towering peaks but also of those who laid rails between those same peaks to carry the riches out to a demanding and insatiable world. The laying of these many rails and the multitude of romantic and cliff-hugging systems they evolved into on the backbone of the continent, especially in the Colorado Rockies, created new dimensions in railroading, chief of which was the vast three-foot-gauge empire and its whole world of equipment, operations and roadbed in a region of breathtaking vistas. Not to be outdone by the glamour of the narrow gauge, the broad-spaced railroaders also pushed and pulled their way in steam over the towering heights to the tune of deafening exhausts and towering plumes of smoke.

All of this was too much to be ignored, and much as the treasure seekers were drawn into the rocky vastness at an earlier date, so too have a score of adventurers, armed with camera and tripod, braved the elements of the high country to record the struggle of the big and the little in steam power at two miles above sea level. To the delight of the rail fraternity their accomplishments have been exhibited in many fine publications over the years and ever so creditably in the works of that dean of rail authors, the late, lamented Lucius Beebe. Names such as Jackson Thode, Otto Perry, John Maxwell, Fred Jukes and a host of others guided by the mountain spirit are spoken with reverence by souls smarting yet from the loss of steam in the high country.

Put to a test it would be hard, if not almost impossible, to single out any one such adventurer in this region. But by considering the years covered in this volume and the unending generosity and unswerving loyalty to all phases of mountain railroading he has demonstrated, we may select one photographer who is a legend in the field. Richard Kindig of Denver, Colorado, is the undisputed king of the mountain. He has roamed the high country since 1934, gathering on film the thunderous and scenic operations of such varied carriers as the Denver and Rio Grande Western in both standard and three-foot gauge, the awe-inspiring ovations of the Union Pacific on famed Sherman Hill and the tranquil wanderings of the old ex-South Park lines. Richard Kindig is a true contemporary pioneer of railroad photography, and it is with great pride that the author presents these samples of his work, which are really far too few in view of the quantity and quality of his self-made collection.

133

Unleashing a smoke plume the like of which will not be seen again in this world — until perhaps Judgment Day — Denver and Rio Grande Western No. 3702, a single-expansion 4-6-6-4 type, climbs the 2.4% grade of Soldier Summit near Kyune, Utah, with 47 progress-resisting box-cars and coal-filled gondolas. A pair of compound articulateds ahead of the caboose shove hard in an all out struggle to make the grade. Even with all this tractive effort the pace is a bare ten miles an hour! (—*Richard Kindig*)

Above In a pose that is as typically Kindig as the felt hat and Graflex in hand, a pair of Union Pacific veterans, 2-10-2 No. 5083 and 4-12-2 No. 9078, beat their way up the east slope of Sherman Hill in Wyoming with 87 cars on a November day in 1947. Despite the almost flat horizon stretching away into the distance this is mountain country, and the grade here at Granite Canyon is 1.55%. Before the hoggers can shove in on the throttle they will have climbed to over 8,000 feet above sea level at the summit in front of the Sherman depot. (*—both, Richard Kindig*)

At left Not all double-shotted drags on the D.&R.G.W. headed for the 2% to Arena, Pinecliff and the Moffat Tunnel. The continuously ascending grade south from Denver to Palmer Lake, the high point on the trackage shared with the Santa Fe and Colorado and Southern to Pueblo, frequently called for helpers on lengthy consists. Literally running along the back fences of Englewood residences, a newly enameled 2-8-8-2 of impressive proportions is helping 4-8-2 No. 1510 get a wheel on 107 cars, the majority of which are empty stock cars destined to move cattle down from the high country before the snow flies.

The horizons on the high plains of eastern Wyoming are endless and the sky is forever, but three-cylindered Union Pacific type No. 9007 is doing its best to blot it all out with a volcanic display of smoke and cinders while beating its way westward near Archer with 102 empty reefers. (*—Richard Kindig*)

Great gray-boilered 4-8-4 No. 820, sans elephant-ear smoke deflectors in this 1949 scene, has topped the stormy summit of Sherman Hill with 15 cars of No. 2, the *Los Angeles Limited*, and rapidly builds up speed on the long downgrade to Cheyenne. Contrastingly colorful in the cloud-etched but still bright sunlight, its consist includes green, yellow and two tan gray again.

Big power, and big smoke, greet the dawn at North Platte, Nebr. Challenger No. 3815 stares into a rising sun it will shortly race toward with an offering of green fruit.

At right It looks cold and it is. Good wintertime photography of steam power in action, with its billowing plumes of steam, spraying snow and the stark contrast of dark machine against the pure white, was not easy to accomplish. The temperamental elements, in creating the much-desired conditions, would contrive to defeat the photographer's efforts with either bitter cold or dark, dreary skies; and in the case of more rural areas, travel to advantageous locations would be downright dangerous. Even once these obstacles had been overcome, a camera lens kept sheltered and then suddenly exposed to low temperatures would coat itself with condensation and, if not detected in time, render all else to no avail. That these obstacles can be surmounted is readily apparent in this scene recorded in northern Idaho in December, 1947, as Union Pacific 2-8-0 No. 284 rolls mixed train No. 386 downgrade along the edge of the almost frozen-over Payette River, just above Smith's Ferry on the old Idaho Northern branch. (*—Richard Kindig*)

Before the influx of high-horsepower Challengers and Big Boy articulateds in the early 1940s, low-drivered drag-era Mallets both simple and compound, all endowed with a Silurian aspect, threaded the crossovers and switches of Tower A at the west end of the Cheyenne yards to begin the attack on the Pleistocene geology of Sherman Hill. Great slithering Mississippian monsters they were, treading ponderously across the switchwork and out onto the slopes of Sherman.

As if in rebuttal to its coming, a strong side wind off Sherman bends the stack exhaust and extra flags distinctly starboard on simple articulated 2-8-8-0 No. 3545, a recent convert from compounding, in this uncluttered scene of 1938. (*—Richard Kindig*)

As surely as Tyrannosaurus rex gave way to generations more fleet of foot and agile in tread, so too did the Silurian drag-era Mallets give way to the higher-drivered, faster-stepping Challengers and Big Boys, which held sway during the peak of steam's reign on the Union Pacific.

Both eastbound and downgrade off the heights of Sherman, a latter-day development from the age of steam, Big Boy No. 4013, spews its innards upon the landscape while drifting effortlessly through the undergrowth of switchwork leading past Tower A and into the same yards whence No. 3545 emerged, on the page opposite, albeit some twenty years earlier. Even this great evolution in steam power was about to be made extinct by yet another creature of the iron age.

On the 3% grade of Raton Pass, three Alco road units, Nos. 55, 56 and 72, roar with the guttural fluctuation that only Alco "PA" power could produce as they lead the 15 cars of No. 19, the *Chief*, up the twisting mountain grade near Wootton, Colo. Giving a more visible assist ahead of the three raging units of internal-combustion power is low-drivered 2-10-2 No. 1680, whose naked trailing truck wheel vies with the drivers themselves in size. (*—Richard Kindig*)

The high plains preceding the mountain elevations were as much a favorite haunt of Kindig and his kind as the rocky heights themselves, especially when spectacles such as this were to be found. The lowering sun has found a gap in the forbidding wall of distant mountains and illuminates completely the undercarriage of two ponderous Colorado and Southern 2-10-2s hoisting a 51-car trainload of wartime freight up the 1.42% grade near Acequia, Colo., in October of 1942 on the Denver-Pueblo run. (—*Richard Kindig*)

SLIM GAUGE JOURNEY

However spectacular standard-gauge railroading in the Rockies may be, with locomotives of impressive proportions and in multiples fore and aft, no mention of Colorado railroading is complete without a reference to the spellbinding operations and methods of the once numerous and now nostalgic three-foot-gauge systems. And no sampling of Mr. Kindig's work could be complete without such a narrow-gauge portfolio as presented here.

Not always were the passenger consists of the narrow-gauge D.&R.G.W. painted the same livid orange as the tourist-carrying Durango-Silverton consist. Traditional Pullman green was once the company standard, and even before that, tuscan red covered the ancient wood sheathing, reminiscent of Pennsylvania Railroad passenger livery. Here in the days of dark green and gold leaf, the last remnant of a multitude of narrow-gauge varnish hauls, the *San Juan* itself — with a full-fledged consist of R.P.O., express cars, coaches and the parlor-observation car Chama — swings both haughtily and hauntingly around a curve east of Durango in the lee of a towering palisade above the Animas River. Outside-frame Mikado No. 473, sporting — albeit dubiously — a fake diamond stack, is still active in steam during the summer, at the head end of the daily Durango-Silverton trip. (*—Richard Kindig*)

Seeming almost to emerge spontaneously out of the rock wall itself, D.&R.G.W. 2-8-0 No. 361 and its seven-car train has just passed through the famous Black Canyon of the Gunnison River, which in this particular view appears to afford little room for a river much less a railroad, even in three-foot gauge. This rendering indicates the reason behind the creation and proliferation of the narrow gauge: canyons and river shelves too narrow for even the relatively small standard gauge steam power of the nineteenth century to tread either physically or economically. No. 361 is en route to the little town of Cimarron, between Gunnison and Montrose, on this June day in 1939. (—*Richard Kindig*)

149

In a scene as hauntingly melancholy as man, machine and the elements could ever hope to achieve, Rio Grande Southern "Mudhen" Mike No. 461, at left, lopes languidly downgrade from the summit of Lizard Head Pass in the San Juan Mountains of southwestern Colorado.

To avoid a collapse of any of the light timber trestles that abounded on the length of the R.G.S., the little 2-8-2 had been cut into the middle of a 13-car northbound extra, where both pulling and pushing she assisted a sister Mudhen, No. 455, in scaling the 3% grade on the south side of the pass. Now in a more relaxed mood she follows the extra's reassembled consist down the north slope. To admirers of this most famous of Colorado narrow-gauge lines the scene is one of both despair and nostalgia, for the date is June, 1951, and within weeks No. 461 and the very rails she rides will be gone forever.

With only days to go before the demise of the entire R.G.S., No. 461, below, is still struggling on the ascent to Lizard Head Pass with a southbound extra of 12 cars into which helper No. 452, on lease from the D.&R.G.W., is sandwiched for safety's sake. (*—Richard Kindig*)

When labor was cheap and the rewards high, painstakingly constructed stone retaining walls, such as this one supporting the weight of Colorado and Southern three-foot-gauge 2-8-0s Nos. 70 and 73, were practical and necessary if the line were to reach the once booming mining camps at the head of every canyon and valley in the front range. In 1938 this retaining wall is showing the effect of frequent slides as the pair of staunch little Consolidations head into Silver Plume, Colo., with seven aging boxcars on one of the last trips of this fabled remnant of the old South Park system. (—*Richard Kindig*)

Not all mountain-slogging steam power was awesome in size or four-cylindered either in compound or in simple. Shay No. 7 of the Klickitat Logging and Lumber Company is multi-cylindered to be sure, but there the resemblance ends. With water bags readily accessible and a generous supply of rerailing frogs handily arranged along the tender frame (which quite possibly hints at some of the day's activities), this stout little work horse is shoving a cut of logs at Reload Camp, some 16 miles northeast of Klickitat, Wash., in 1964.

As the Colorado Rockies once echoed with the sounds of the Rogers, the Cookes, the Masons and the Mudhens, so too did the timbered slopes of the Northwest echo with the rapid-fire exhausts of these lopsided log maulers, but as if by mutual consent they too have disappeared from the mountain fastness. (*—Hank Griffiths*)

Mallet articulateds of impressive proportions were not confined to operations on the grades of the U.P. or the Rio Grande. Transcontinentals laboring over the continental divide further north also thrust their tonnage against the western slopes behind such behemoths as the Great Northern's massive 2-8-8-2 No. 2046 heading west out of Minot, N.Dak., with 75 cars of regular-carded redball No. 40. (—*Fred Sankoff*)

However, one fact was readily apparent to the photographer accustomed to the steady and seemingly never-ending parade of big-time steam on the Union Pacific main across Wyoming: they just didn't run that way on the single-track lines of the G.N. or Northern Pacific. A wait of several hours could be encountered before recording such a scene as N.P. Challenger No. 5146 creates near Rapids Siding, Mont., rushing 114 cars east at 60 an hour. Photographer Hank Griffiths, of U.P. Blue Mountain fame, relates that this photograph is mute evidence of another frustration in recording N.P. steam power: burning rosebud coal, of a finer grade than the lignite used by the paralleling carriers to the south, the locomotives could not produce that much-coveted volcanic plume of smoke billowing, say, from the double stack of a U.P. Big Boy.

The Western Pacific was generally regarded as a mountain climber of a railroad, and justifiably so in view of its famed Feather River Canyon climb and the Keddie wye and engine terminal in the towering California Sierra, where motive power of spectacular proportions was prevalent, such as Mallet No. 201, which sits simmering next to the Keddie enginehouse between helper assignments. However, Western Pacific's management was more disposed to roll the system's freight behind an uncommonly well-proportioned group of Mikado types over the long, undulating and relatively menial elevations of the Nevada-Utah desert. Regardless of their aesthetic attributes the 40 engines of this class were seldom shown in print, but thanks to Richard Kindig, who crossed over the mountains on a September day in 1950, we here find a pair of these rarities blasting their way up a yard lead into the joint W.P.-D.&R.G.W. yards at Salt Lake City, Utah. The 80 or so cars they have just rolled across the saline flats of the Great Salt Lake basin in short order will be hoisted up to Soldier Summit by a pair of impressive Rio Grande articulateds. (*—Richard Kindig*)

Denver and Rio Grande Western 4-8-4 No. 1710 crosses the Colorado River at Glenwood Springs, Colo., in September of 1938 with third No. 2, an American Legion special running as a section of the once popular, tourist-laden *Scenic Limited*. Ironically, not only has the train succumbed to the tourist's new-found love for the automobile, but the bridge itself has been removed and replaced further downstream in deference to a newly constructed Interstate highway. (*—Richard Kindig*)

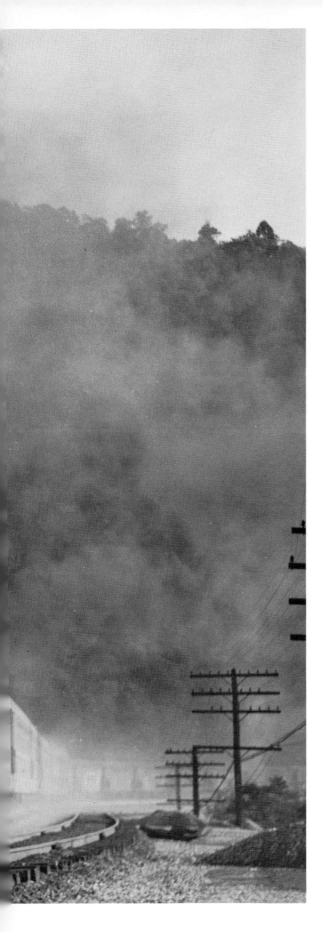

In stark contrast to Mr. Kindig's Colorado railroad coverage is this view of the Baltimore and Ohio's blue-painted and streamlined Pacific No. 5302, striding up Cranberry Grade in West Virginia at a brisk 35 an hour with No. 76, the *Cincinnatian*. This pleasant surprise in the Kindig file results from one of his rare trips away from the high country.

Despite 80-inch drivers and a consist of deceptively streamlined equipment, which in reality were all converted heavyweights, No. 5302 and her sister engines seldom if ever required a helper to make the grade. (*—Richard Kindig*)

Photographer Kindig readily admits that his forays beyond the mountainous railroading of the West were somewhat less than infrequent — a matter of one or two, to be exact — and even these for some inexplicable reason resulted in trips to the mountain country of West Virginia and the famous Cranberry grade of the Baltimore and Ohio, where Mallet articulateds of a size and frequency akin to spectacles once witnessed on Tennessee Pass in mid-Colorado were much to his liking. Thus, in addition to the foregoing work of Mr. Kindig, we find B.&O. EM-1 2-8-8-4

No. 7612 clawing its way up the west slope of Cranberry near Terra Alta, W.Va., at a steady 15 miles an hour with freight No. 96. Then, by 64 cars to the rear and showing their efforts more visually than does No. 7612 up front, a pair of helpers obliterate the sky with soft-coal smoke as eight sets of cylinders alternate between push and pull. Immediately behind the caboose is No. 7133, a single-expansion 2-8-8-0, followed by No. 7047, a true Mallet compound 0-8-8-0.

With the race nearly won, brightly polished Pacific No. 1015 sprints through the slip switches of the Lenox interlocker at Mitchell, Ill., with the silhouetted St. Louis skyline faintly visible in the hogger's eyes. From here on into the St. Louis station sheds the rails are all jointly used, with crisscrossing traffic patterns allowing the dapper little train to regain its breath after rolling like the proverbial hammers of Hades to avoid throwing yellow caution blocks in front of a mighty New York Central Hudson, making up time with an already behind-schedule second section of the similarly St. Louis-bound *Southwestern Limited*. (—C. E. Prusia)

10. Zip, Zip, Went the C. & E. I. Zipper

Zip, Zip, goes the Chicago and Eastern Illinois *Zipper,* a delightful run in steam days long gone. The *Zipper* was a minute capsule of all the bigness of the named runs on four-track mains, made even more endearing to the eye by the silvered cylinder heads, red-painted number plates, graphite smokeboxes and Cyclopean headlights of what was certainly the most meticulously polished and maintained little group of Pacific types to grace the rails of any steam road, large or small.

Using a longer route through less populated areas than its competition on the St. Louis-Chicago haul, the little *Zipper* was a poor fourth cousin to such runs as the *Bluebird, Green Diamond* and *Ann Rutledge* in revenue gathered aboard. Undaunted by that fact, the intrepid little *Zipper* actually outran its competition with sheer speed in order to maintain and advertise a competing schedule between the two midwestern cities. Lacking direct access to St. Louis at the end of the run, the *Zipper* was obliged to use the leased rails of the New York Central's Big Four route as far as Pana, Illinois, a feature that required it to travel in an east-west direction before it could swing into the true north-south route that was demanded and enjoyed by competing runs. Mathematicians would describe the *Zipper* as running up the sides of a right triangle while its competition used the hypotenuse.

On occasion when the mighty New York Central's St. Louis-bound *Southwestern Limited* was a few minutes behind schedule, the *Zipper's* abbreviated consist would be allowed on the leased iron at Pana for the last lap into St. Louis ahead of the high-stepping, Hudson-powered Central speedster, and a race akin to that of the hare and the tortoise was on. The brightly polished but lower-drivered little 4-6-2 literally had to run itself to death to stay ahead of the racing Hudson closing in behind it. One of the most thrilling moments of this race usually occurred at Hillsboro, Illinois, where the harried little train would duck beneath the huge coal dock and slow to a stop at the station platform just long enough to set down a detraining passenger and gulp down a tankful of much-needed water, and then with ever-increasing stack talk the little Pacific would roar back into motion, disappearing rapidly into the lowering sun. A moment later, with a swiftness that shocked the onlooker, that mighty Central Hudson, its whistle screaming and with wind-whipped remnants of green flags atop its smokebox front, would literally explode from under the same coal dock and, rather than making a station stop, tear by the depot at nearly ninety an hour and disappear with a cloud of dust and coal smoke into the same slightly lowered sun. One could only stand in wonderment for moments after.

Left Sprightly speedster, lean and racy C.&E.I. Pacific No. 1004 chomps at the bit, waiting on the St. Louis Union Station leads to lock couplers with the abbreviated consist of the northbound *Zipper* haul on a summer morning in the mid-1940s. The term "abbreviated" is here used only in comparison with the more lengthy consists of the competing trains on the St. Louis-Chicago hauls; the *Zipper* itself was a minute but complete capsule of all that any cross-country name train could offer, with a heavyweight R.P.O., coach, full diner, and a combination Pullman-lounge-solarium bringing up the rear. (—R. J. Foster)

Below Second No. 11, the all-Pullman section of the *Southwestern Limited*, rattles the boards of the depot platform at Hillsboro, Ill., in its race with time and the Pennsy's *Spirit of St. Louis* on a competitive route further south, as it roars from under the big concrete coal dock at 90 an hour. The C.&E.I.'s *Zipper* has been out-flanked this day; both sections of the *Southwestern* are running on schedule and close enough together that the less-prestigous little train will have to content itself with following behind Hudson No. 5389.

The author once looked with horror at this very scene in 1945. A large week-end crowd of patrons was awaiting the St. Louis-bound *Zipper*, and upon hearing a train whistle east of the coal dock, they all emerged from the depot and arrayed themselves and their luggage dangerously near the rails, only to look up in astonishment and see, not the *Zipper* slowing to a halt, but a scene such as this. The hogger's frantic yanking at the whistle and waving his hand in a "get back" motion prevented a tragedy.

The petunias in bloom, the whitewashed tree trunks and well-trimmed lawn are a scene as much a bygone memory as the steam locomotive itself! (—*Walter Peters*)

Left With the towers of the Pennsy's Chicago River lift bridge for a backdrop, No. 1004 is away at the other end of the run as it clatters over the busy 21st Street crossing in Chicago, not with the *Zipper* but with its short-lived successor, the *Cardinal*. Incongruously its consist was not painted the obvious bright-red, equivalent of its namesake bird's gay plumage, but, in keeping with the adopted color pattern of the C.&E.I.'s first diesels, the cars were an ultramarine blue, heavily striped with bright orange. Because of failing demand for its better accommodations, on a route with few opulent patrons, the *Zipper* was discontinued in 1947 and replaced with the *Cardinal*, which operated on virtually the same schedule but with more mediocre equipment, as is witnessed here: two coaches and a combination buffet-Pullman.

The *Cardinal's* consist also fell prey to the general decline in passenger traffic and it was discontinued in 1949, leaving the way free for the Central's *Southwestern Limited*, now more often behind a diesel electric than a mighty Hudson, to go its way without fear of finding this foreign-line intruder just a few signal blocks ahead. (—*James Konas*)

Dusting the roadbed with soft-coal smoke in a hasty passage akin to that of its northern relative on the St. Louis-Chicago run, C.&E.I. Atlantic No. 222 exhibits all the traits of the *Zipper* itself as it scurries south near Marion, Ill., with the daily varnish run, the only passenger service on a segment of the C.&E.I. system more accustomed to U.S.R.A. Mikados trundling coal drags and empty hoppers back and forth than to the canted cylinders and red-painted number plate of No. 222.

Exhibiting somewhat less urgency in its passage than No. 5389 on a page previous, bug-spattered New York Central Hudson No. 5385 has just filled its tender bunker at the Hillsboro, Ill., coal dock and now with the sharp stack exhaust once so familiar to Hudson admirers is urging an eight-car express and head-end revenue train, running as an advance section of the *Southwestern*, back into motion for the final lap to the St. Louis station sheds. Extra sections such as this, with little more than minutes of headway between the runs, made it even more difficult for the Central dispatcher to sneak the *Zipper* onto the leased trackage.

Let it be said to their credit that folks in the coal country were never too busy to look up as a train went by. M-1 Berkshire No. 1985 receives rapt attention from a pair of onlookers as it storms upgrade into Norton, Va., in 1949. A symbol of steam now as distant as the steam locomotive itself, a fat, wooden water-storage tank sits hulking at trackside, silent witness to many such stirring spectacles in the coal country. (*—August A. Thieme, Jr.*)

11. *The Old Reliable and Friends*

Awakening to the fact that the largest, ever-changing billboard display in the world was at their disposal in the form of a moving freight train, rail managements after World War II moved en masse to emblazon boxcar sides with what was fervently hoped would be revenue-creating slogans. Many used phrases already identifiable with the carrier such as "All the way on the Santa Fe," while others flatly commanded the producer to "Ship it on the Frisco," or "Be specific — ship Union Pacific." In the bluegrass country of Kentucky, however, the railroad most strongly associated with that state and especially with its bountiful coal traffic, the Louisville and Nashville, surprised no one with a choice of slogans that was both appropriate to the carrier's conservative ways and fitted to the slow-paced life of the middle South. The "Old Reliable" was just that.

Not given to shouting its own merits or shocking the railroad world with wild experimental innovations, the L.&N. went its way in the years of steam almost solely dependent upon a roster of World War I United States Railroad Administration designs. Light and heavy Mikados were the mainstay of its freight roster, while light Pacific and Mountain types were its standard passenger power, and as if this were not enough, the freight yards resounded to the bark of U.S.R.A. 0-8-0s kicking the cars down the leads.

Except for a venture into three-cylinder power with a Pacific and a Mikado in 1927, which proved to the Old Reliable as it did to others sampling the American Locomotive Company's offerings that the extra maintenance just wasn't worth it, the L.&N.'s first really new steam power came to the road in 1944 in the form of twenty M-1 class 2-8-4s, at once a notably aesthetic and impressive design. Increased by 22 more such engines from Lima Locomotive in 1949, the entire roster went to work hauling 8,000-ton coal drags out of such appropriately named mining towns as Hazard, Corbin, Ravenna, Appalachia and Cumberland; all these trains were destined for the huge DeCoursey classification yard, just south of Cincinnati, Ohio.

Meanwhile, back in Louisville, the Old Reliable's base camp, the M-1s were an infrequent sight, appearing only for heavy shopping in the south Louisville shops or on Derby Day, when the loads of patrons for the famous event were a little much for the light U.S.R.A. power. Outside of these instances, the more timeworn motive power was the rule, and indeed such was also the case with other carriers sharing the Louisville scene with the Old Reliable. Located on divisions other than the main line, the more modern and impressive locomotives were seldom, if ever, seen in Louisville terminals, while the venerable and aged steeds handled the brunt of traffic to Whisky Town.

Until the advent of the M-1 Berkshires, the L.&N.'s primary freight movers and the locomotives most closely associated with the Old Reliable's steam image were the J-4 class Mikados. Their importance is attested to by the road's owning 165 of this class engine, the largest single group on the roster. Other than the addition of Worthington S.A.E. feedwater heaters, all essentially retained the original U.S.R.A. look. With big boilers and headlights of like proportions, they were an extremely photogenic locomotive, good-looking from every angle.

Above, at the Louisville enginehouse, a covey of the dirty-chinned, all-business, no-horseplay machines sits out on a Sunday afternoon, a not uncommon sight when traffic felt the lack of week-end carloadings. (—*Jack Fravert*)

Anticipating a slip of the drivers upon starting, the hogger of the Louisville and Nashville's 4-6-2 No. 232 grinds to a halt with sanders open at St. Matthews, Ky., the first stop out of Louisville for the Lexington-bound local. The station agent and baggage man begin a hasty exchange of business in this 1950 scene that will be repeated many times before No. 20 on the L.&N.'s time-table ends its 94-mile run in the bluegrass center. No. 232 is a product of the L.&N.'s own shops in 1915 and carries the same locomotive classification as the Pennsylvania's famed K-4s Pacifics. (*—Jack Fravert*)

Below Silhouetted against a cloud of steam of its own making, and with blower roaring, a work-scarred veteran of the Pennsylvania Railroad, B6s 0-6-0 No. 7977, grabs a few minutes leisure time on the open-stall tracks of the Louisville 14th Street round-house in 1952. (*—Jack Fravert*)

A study in grime. Making sharply visible every part of its undercarriage, an accumulation of finely ground sand covers drivers, rods and piping alike on M-1 No. 1991 awaiting its turn for servicing on the inbound engine lead at DeCoursey, Ky. Swirled upwards by the motion of the wheels and rods, accumulations such as this were common to the work-a-day appearance of these robust locomotives and indicate the grades and tonnage to which they were assigned. Replenishing this sand supply was wholly as important as fueling and watering; M-1 No. 1966 sits patiently under the DeCoursey coal dock while the hostler's helper fills the cavernous dome with the white stuff. The grimy tonnage mover is beginning to show the ravages of poor maintenance and hard work in this 1956 scene and is not long from joining the rows of dead brethren near-by awaiting the cutting torch. (—*Jack Fravert*)

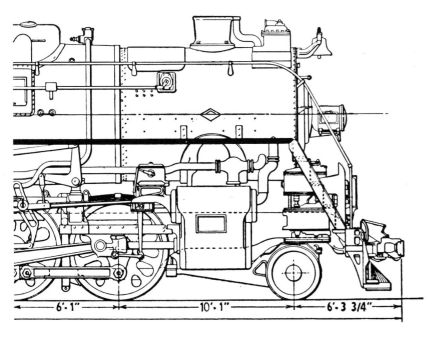

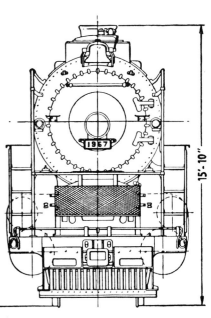

Above The air is full of smoke and the sounds of steam at Ravenna, Ky., and M-1 No. 1972 adds to the tumult while taking a ride on the engine-house turntable in search of a stall.

Below Less tumult and less engine. Its ancestry obviously L.&N., a gun-barrel-boilered 2-6-0 of the Flemingsburg and Northern sighs contentedly on a warm October morning while waiting to leave its home port of Flemingsburg, Ky., with the daily mixed. (*—Jack Fravert*)

Even the Chesapeake and Ohio reached a long, slim finger out of Ashland, Ky., through Lexington and into Louisville; like other first-class carriers that elected to journey to Derby Town, the line's management assigned its older and lighter power to the single-track route. In the C.&O.'s case this meant Pacific types such as No. 435, swinging with the *Fast Flying Virginian* through the reverse curve and onto the Louisville-Cincinnati line of the L.&N. at Tower HK near Anchorage, Ky. Later in the evening No. 435 will put in an appearance once again with the *F.F.V.'s* eastbound counterpart, the *Sportsman.* (—*Jack Fravert*)

Amid the still-brown countryside in the early spring of 1953, PS-2 No. 1231 of the Southern was the only green thing in sight as she climbed the 4% grade west of New Albany, Ind., on the Louisville-St. Louis line. The engine crew will soon slam shut the cab windows for the trip through the mile-long Duncan Tunnel at the top of the grade. At the time of this exposure the Louisville-to-Princeton, Ind., train rated an asterisk in the Southern's passenger timetable as the only exception to an all diesel-powered schedule. Alas, by the end of this same spring, No. 1231 and her sister, No. 1317 (which made the last run), had disappeared; and so ended the last regular run of the Southern's green-and-gold steamers. (—*Jack Fravert*)

Emerging almost reptilelike from its lair, the Baltimore and Ohio's President-class Pacific No. 5301 eases abruptly around the sharp curve in front of the New Albany, Ind., depot and out onto the public street prior to climbing the approach to the Ohio River bridge. No. 5301 is making one of the last steam runs on the Cincinnati-Louisville passenger service in 1956. (*—Jack Fravert*)

A pair of the L&N.'s favorite reliables, J-4 class Mikados, round the curve at Anchorage, Ky., with Cincinnati-bound freight in 1950. (—*Jack Fravert*)

If you didn't know the names of the L.&N.'s fast-freight runs, you might think the freshly applied gilt copy on the side of this auxiliary water car trailing heavy Mike No. 1760 was a rolling advertisement for the legendary masked man of radio broadcasting's heyday. The stubby tank car was used to extend the distance between water stops for the carrier's freight power.

Louisville and Nashville steam power was never a favorite among rail photographers, obviously due to the line's minimal effort toward cleanliness and visible maintenance. No. 1183, an elderly work horse of the Old Reliable, has just emerged from the shops with new cylinder packing, repairs and a new coat of paint — but only on the cylinders.

(—top, Louisville & Nashville R.R.)
(—bottom, Jack Fravert)

Why alter a tried and proven method, especially when the results are such as this? A rarity both for the day it was operated and in its manner of operation, the first triple-headed steam-powered fan trip in Canada, a York Railroad Preservation Society run of 14 cars between Toronto and Orangeville, steams grandly into camera focus near Alton, Ont., in May of 1960 behind the splendiferous side motions of Canadian Pacific 4-4-0 No. 136, and 4-6-0s Nos. 1057 and 815. The sight of the doughty little American type in the lead is enough to soften the heart of every steam lover, be he an adherent of the wedgie or some more radical form of railroad photography. (—*Fred Sankoff*)

12. Canada's Own, a Perfectionist with the Flying Wedge

The "wedge," the "wedgie" and "pie-shaped" were terms that came into general use during the last days of steam operations for describing the orthodox, generally accepted, stopped-in-motion view of an oncoming train, or in more simple terms, the shape evolved as the train approached the camera. This is opposed to the views of the latter-day school of rail photographers employing the telescopic look, the panned and blurred-at-speed appearance, and generally speaking, the distorted look — compelling a train to look like anything but an approaching train. We can credit these creative photographers with some really unusual and provocative film records of steam or diesels at work, and such views seem indicative of the times: radical distortions, not necessarily for the better. Regardless of the viewpoint, the wedge or three-quarter view of an oncoming train once was *the* accepted pose for photographers the country over, and all employed it to its best advantage. With the train approaching from the distance in a perspective plane and itself creating a point in perspective, what better way to show the train, the entire train from the pilot point to the far-distant caboose, than to let it form at the appropriate moment a true wedge of machinery on the move across the undulating topography?

The above artistic reasoning was all an established fact to Fred Sankoff of Toronto, Ontario, who strove for perfection in the technique of the wedge-shaped action view. Such efforts were not new to the railroad photographic fraternity, for after all, pioneer and professional alike have recorded the view for years. However, Mr. Sankoff's requirements were uncompromising: clear, uncluttered backgrounds were a must; tangents in open, level terrain were his forte; the embellishment of a smoke plume heightened the feeling of movement and action; but above all he demanded the proper stage on which to record his wedge-shaped masterpieces. A native of Canada, and like all railroad cameramen having a normal partiality to carriers in his home area, Mr. Sankoff can boast of one of the finest and most complete collections of Canadian steam railroad photography in existence, all of his own making. It is somewhat ironic, but not altogether unusual in the photo fraternity, that while he could have vaulted into the United States with ease and ferreted out steam in the deep valleys of near-by New York and Pennsylvania, this adherent to perfection chose instead to make long journeys to the far western reaches of Canada, where in the flat, boundless horizons of Manitoba and Saskatchewan he found settings to his liking. There on the wide-open prairies of the wheat provinces a train could be seen in progress for miles before ever coming within camera range, and then it would come both straight and level. Without encroachment upon the right of way by tenements, industry or other signs of civilization, and with the elements themselves not given kindly to the growth of rail-hiding weeds, the settings were perfect for Fred Sankoff's needs.

This is not to say that photographer Sankoff ignored the railroads south of his border. Indeed not, for his wedge-shaped masterpieces include many a scene in the latter days of U.S. steam operations. However, the author will testify that to accompany this perfection-bound photographer on one of his Stateside safaris means that one must be stout of heart and strong of wind. Always in search of a clearer background and less clutter at trackside, cameraman Sankoff was wont to quit the more easily accessible locations and strike out via rutted roads or on foot to attain his desires, sometimes with little regard for his own safety. However, he readily admits that after recording the scene of Canadian National No. 5131 leaving Reditt, Ontario, on the pages following, the warnings heard earlier in the day of hungry bears in the immediate area, into which he had hiked for this shot, served to increase both his gait and his perspiration as he recovered the mile across country to his parked auto.

The more lately conceived 4-8-4 wheel arrangement may have been the dual-service machine of Stateside railroads, but in the provinces of Canada the vintage 4-6-2 arrangement was the dual-purpose motive power in every respect. Amassed in considerable quantities by both of the Canadian transcontinentals, the proven design was to be found nearly everywhere, performing every conceivable task assigned to railroad motive power.

With a fire hot enough to set the safety valves popping, Canadian National 4-6-2 No. 5572 is working as helper engine ahead of 4-8-4 No. 6121 as together they bring a westward extra up Dunden Hill and by the Bayview Tower near Hamilton, Ont. (—*Fred Sankoff*)

Chalk up one more for the photographer. Rarely photographed in action, and never in so excellent a pose, one of the only two Northern types ever to grace the rails of the Canadian Pacific puts on a near perfect show of smoke and steam as it heads a drag freight east over the pool-table terrain between Brandon and Winnipeg, Manitoba, in the summer of 1957.

As one might suspect, request was made beforehand for that magnificent plume of oil smoke, and yet many miles of frantic pacing by auto along the transcontinental highway, with frequent tire-screeching halts at potentially favorable locations, were required before just the right view was recorded. (*—Fred Sankoff*)

"Mtys" west in the Far North. This length of wooden reefers, with their ice hatches pointing skyward, is more reminiscent of scenes along the U.P.'s right of way during the green-fruit season. Canadian National 4-8-2 No. 6002 has just been converted from coal to oil-burning in the Stratford, Ont., shops and shows proof of the event in an outpouring of thick, black clouds of smoke, as oil-burners are wont to do, as she heads for an assignment in the western provinces, bringing 80 empty, red C.N. reefers and a few assorted boxcars with her. Recorded near Searle, Manitoba, in July, 1958. (—Fred Sankoff)

The sun comes up bright and early out west in the wheat provinces and what better way to start the day? It was an early 6:30 a.m. in July, 1959, when photographer Sankoff recorded this pluperfect wedgie of Canadian National 2-8-2 No. 3590 hustling time freight No. 412 east into Saskatoon, Saskatchewan. (Fred Sankoff)

Forming a wedgie, although much abbreviated, heavy-browed Consolidation No. 2464 of the Duluth, Winnipeg and Pacific sports a Coffin feedwater heater mounted outside and in front of its soot-encrusted smokebox as it lopes downhill toward the Duluth, Minn., yards after assisting a sister 2-8-0 up the heavy northbound grade with a freight headed for the parent Canadian National main line at Winnipeg. The high-cupolaed, orange-painted caboose tags along in deference to union rulings that with a three-man crew there be shelter for the one off duty. (*—Fred Sankoff*)

One would presume from the foregoing photographs that our expert of the flying wedge devoted his talents entirely to the transcontinental twosome of Canada, but such was not the case. Conspicuous by their absence from the printed pages of a multitude of railroad publications, the only two Berkshire types in all Canada, those of the Toronto, Hamilton and Buffalo, came in for their share of Mr. Sankoff's attention. Judging from their lack of publicity, action photographs of either of these two rarities are almost nonexistent, except for such gems as the one pictured here.

The author has always felt it a shame that so little record of this singularly beautiful locomotive's existence can be found. Exhibiting the tendencies of its parent road, the New York Central, in its compact, angular design and yet free from clearance limitations, as is most Canadian steam power, this two-of-a-kind rare breed was, not too surprisingly, sired by the test results on a similar wheel arrangement, a 1400 class original Lima superpower creation, on yet another N.Y.C. subsidiary, the Boston and Albany.

The great clouds of white smoke and steam spewing forth from the innards of No. 202 attest to the photographer's statement that it was a raw and bitter-cold March day as the engine faced into a strong wind with an extra headed east out of Welland, Ont., for the yards at Niagara Falls over the rails of the Central's Canada Southern Division. (*—Fred Sankoff*)

186

Outside of poison ivy or snakebite, a rail photographer venturing into even the remotest areas of the United States has little to be concerned with in the way of nature's potential enemies, but the story can be different in some of the wild and remote parts of the Canadian provinces, where several varieties of carnivorous wildlife still exist. The desire for just one more perfect photograph overshadowed the warnings of the head-end crew on Canadian National 4-6-2 No. 5131, about to leave Redditt, Ont., with mixed run No. 214 for Sioux Lookout. When the photographer requested lots of smoke for several miles after leaving town, since he planned to hike into the heavily wooded area for a shot truly indicative of the run, the crew advised him about the number of bears, hungry and mean from their months of winter hibernation, that had been spotted in the vicinity. Not until Mr. Sankoff had bagged this scene of railroading in the wild and started his long hike back to town did the hogger's warning take hold; no bears were encountered, but his pace and pulse both quickened rapidly as he covered the last mile in record time! *(—Fred Sankoff)*

Southwestbound at sunup, a disc-drivered Mountain type of the St. Louis-San Francisco cracks the whip with mixed tonnage at Pacific, Mo., in 1940. (—*Ivan Oaks*)

13. Gems of the Southwest

It was a logical circumstance that the heavily populated Northeast, Midwest and West Coast areas should have spawned the greatest numbers of rail buffs and railroad photographers because of their numerous and wide-ranging systems. Considering also the prosperity of a given geographic area, it is unlikely that the rugged, oak-grown hills of Tennessee or Arkansas would support individuals with a zest for such an expensive and time-consuming hobby, when most residents earn not much more than a bare livelihood, compared to the relative affluence of the commercial East and North. Thus we find whole geographic areas and their accompanying railroad systems that have largely been neglected by photographers during the tenure of steam motive power.

This is especially unfortunate since many of the carriers in these areas endowed their operations with an unhurried cordiality and their equipment with a personal touch which, when once experienced, endeared them forever to the traveler. Performing their operations with less urgency and concern than was habitual with larger and more opulent carriers in the impatient and unfeeling East, where railroading was more a job than a pleasure, the more isolated systems took time to add embellishments that would still be their trademark long after the steam locomotive had ceased to be.

Witness the distinguishing red-and-white trademark of the Missouri-Kansas Texas Railroad prominently displayed on the sides of every locomotive tender. This singular emblem did more to establish the Katy in the traveler's mind than any other appurtenance. Although the system's roster was comprised of sightly and graceful engines in the smaller-sized wheel arrangements, the largest power being Mikados and Pacifics, one could hardly find a group of more austere and generally uncluttered locomotives. Completely bereft of the adornments and appliances generally taken for granted by road foremen on other railroads, Katy steam power possessed the graceful and light-of-limb appearance befitting a famous race horse. Bulging feedwater heaters and accompanying piping were nonexistent on Katy superstructures, lending a clean, uncluttered look to switchers and road power alike.

Former Katy engine crews are quick to point out that the cab backheads were as absent of controls as the exteriors were of things to be controlled. The technical-minded may point out that the ton-miles and tonnage ratings suffered from the lack of such improvements, but one would be hard put to agree, after witnessing the once commonplace ninety and hundred-car drags and redballs that were hustled across the Southwest behind the austere flanks of the Katy's biggest. Be that as it may, whether by choice or by chance Katy steam power was one more rare and beautiful jewel in the collection of southwestern United States railroad motive power, a jewel box that included such gems as the Texas and Pacific, Kansas City Southern, Cotton Belt, St. Louis-San Francisco, Missouri Pacific and that trio of Midland Valley legend: the Oklahoma City-Ada-Atoka, the Kansas, Oklahoma and Gulf and the namesake Midland Valley itself.

While certain parts of Texas and Oklahoma did blossom with wealth from oil wells and agriculture, the Southwest was generally a poor area devoid of native photographers who would preserve the comings and goings of the aforementioned carriers. Thus with few exceptions the credit for this "jewel box" goes largely to two gentlemen of the Southwest: Preston George of Oklahoma City and R. S. Plummer of Sulphur Springs, Texas. Both of these men possessed a love of the steam locomotive and the determination to preserve its existence on film, ingredients needed in quantity where long trips over great distances were accompanied by long waits for sometimes infrequent schedules. The jewels that follow are mute testimony to their efforts.

Their exhausts, unimpeded by detours through feedwater heaters and sundry other piping, resound not unlike a continuous artillery barrage as two big-boiled Mikes of the Katy rampage through Wagoner, Okla., with 145 cars of mixed tonnage.
(—*Johnnie Gray*)

There was no mistaking Katy steam power wherever it operated, whether in one of the three states whose initials formed part of the brilliant heraldry displayed so prominently on the tender flanks of its motive power, or in the Sooner State, whose "O." was conspicuous by its absence from the corporate insignia. One did not have to be an expert on Katy steam power: one eyeful of that bright red-and-white emblem displayed on yard and road power alike was identification enough, in the busy Kansas City terminal or high on the horizon of the Oklahoma panhandle.

Bright and sightly in fresh enamel and displaying proudly the herald of which we speak, a pair of spirited Katy Moguls in 1948 lope across western Oklahoma near Altus with a lengthy 41-car grain extra destined for Gulf-port shipping docks.

(—Preston George)

191

Unmistakably a Missouri-Kansas-Texas creation, from its slotted sheet-metal
pilot and white-trimmed drivers and running boards to the Katy shield on
its tender and encores of the same shield on every head-end revenue car in
the consist, the carrier's own *Katy Limited* rolls impressively down the
double-track iron near Stringtown, Okla., in 1948. As if all the aforementioned identification were not enough, midway in the consist rolls one of
the Katy's own characteristic bright-yellow express boxcars, which were
carried in most of the road's first-class hauls during and immediately after
the height of the Katy's steam operations. (*—Preston George*)

192

A rare gem this? Beauty is in the eye of the beholder, and if the beholder is a true fan of the Burlington look then a gem is beheld. With a rivet-studded air reservoir tucked under her chin, a flat-faced, high-headlighted old dowager of a 4-6-2, Fort Worth and Denver F-3-A class No. 551, shows she can still turn a mean wheel despite her 28 years of hard labor under the Texas sun as she rolls speedily and smokily out of Dallas with Ft. Worth-bound No. 2, the *Texas Zephyr*. (—R. S. Plummer)

A road of contrasts in steam power, the Kansas City Southern was accustomed to coupling together some rather incongruous lash-ups when tonnage and grades demanded more than a single locomotive could deliver. Highly unlikely combinations were not uncommon, as evidenced by high-stepping, multi-domed Pacific No. 808 hurrying warily ahead of a ponderous 2-10-4, No. 905, as they gather momentum on the downgrade out of Page, Okla., with 65 empty hoppers.

On the page opposite another doubleheader of unusual proportions is having a rougher time of it battling the uphill side of the grade into Page with a drag of like tonnage. A low-drivered, squat 2-8-0 uses an auxiliary water car to hold at bay a hulking monster of a 2-8-8-0, which by itself is turning day into night with a thunderous exhaust that threatens to obliterate the surrounding countryside.

Early in the diesel era the K.C.S. perpetuated its reputation for the unusual in motive power combinations by hooking up heretofore unheard-of multitudes of A and B units, obviously to eliminate helper service on the Ozark grades, against which its onetime steam power is here shown struggling. (—both, *Preston George*)

194

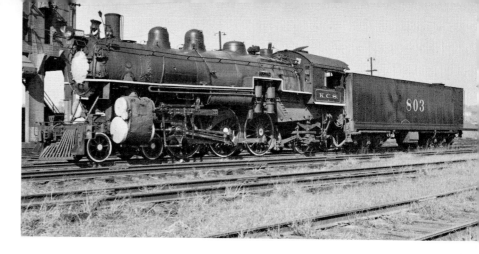

Shades of the Santa Fe! Borrowing the boxcar-sized tender concept from the big transcontinental, the little K.C.S. put together this box-shaped monster and coupled it to a 1912-built Pacific in the '30s to allow less frequent stops for fuel and water on the road's then first-class passenger haul, the *Flying Crow*. Veteran Pacific No. 803, the dubious recipient of this gargantua of tenders, waits on the Kansas City Terminal's leads before backing down to the sheds for the *Crow* itself. Little else of significance was effected in stylizing No. 803 for its assigned service, other than to cover the cylinder heads and smokebox door with aluminum paint, but then with that singularly distinctive tender what else was needed? (*—Robert J. Foster*)

MIDLAND VALLEY

Midland Valley is a railroad name as general in its location and nearly as legendary as the famed Happy Valley line of hobo lore. The railroad was one of a trio of lines radiating out of Muskogee, Oklahoma, to the north, west and south, and the motive power of the combined systems carried full identification of the entire threesome on their tender sides: Midland Valley; Kansas, Oklahoma and Gulf; and the Oklahoma City-Ada-Atoka Railway.

As the author had not yet seen this threesome, they were a "must" stop on a journey into the Southwest in 1951. Accordingly, the meticulously maintained enginehouse at Muskogee was located, examined and found to be bulging with such various goodies as tiered-dome Mikados with straight boilers of lean diameter, tapered main rods and multiple-guide crossheads, and fat and squat Consolidations, reminiscent of power once viewed on Marshall Pass and Lizard Head, while near-by the blower roared

on a lean-limbed and racy Santa Fe type. All this was too much for the author, who crept stealthily from cover to cover recording every item of power left outside. Without official permission on his person and too anxious to spend time obtaining it, this photographer had decided on the subversive style of approach, still chafing from an unceremonious heave-ho from the property of the Tremont and Gulf Railway only the day before. In short order, after covering every item of motive power in sight and feeling very smug about it all, this would-be secret agent turned to leave and literally collided with a large and obviously official individual who asked if the author wanted to photograph the steam engines. To the photographer's utter amazement and delight, this impressive gentleman, who turned out to be the system superintendent of motive power, ordered all the locomotives out of the house, across the turntable and into an advantageous position, where this ex-undercover agent could record them to his pleasure.

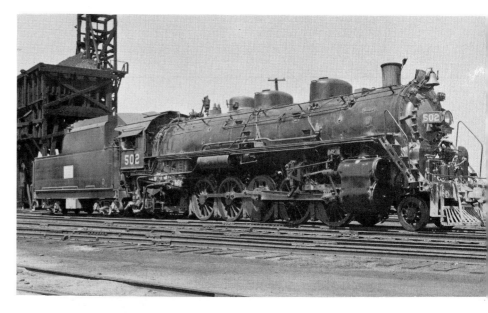

196

Two more irresistible examples of Midland Valley power are shown here out of Muskogee. Handsomely styled U.S.R.A. Mikado No. 94 with a lengthy hotshot heads north, while an affectionate little hound of a Consolidation scurries across the Okie countryside. Note the unusual round metal markers, for daytime use, above the marker lamps of No. 233, a style peculiar to this little trio of carriers. (*—Preston George*)

Sulphur Springs, in northeast Texas, is not only the home of R. S. Plummer, who has proven his talent as a gem collector of southwestern steam power, but it also is the home of the Carnation Belt, Sulphur Bluff and Pacific Railroad, of which Mr. Plummer, as manager of the Carnation Milk plant there, is president, regardless of the fact the plant railroad is only 1,000 feet in length. Sulphur Springs is also on the main iron of the St. Louis-Southwestern Railroad, whose operations total some 1,000 miles in length. Bring all this together and we have here R. S. Plummer's magnificent rendering of the Cotton Belt's first No. 343, the *Blue Streak Fast Freight,* rolling west into the setting sun with 4-8-4 No. 809 making stack music at the helm. The head-end crew not only has a clear board atop the order mast but gets an extra highball wave from some of the local citizenry.

The Cotton Belt has always been a wonder and a mystery to the author because, either by chance or by choice, its operations department bypassed those accepted American standards in steam locomotives, the Mikado and Pacific, completely and instead persisted in hauling its

freight and passengers behind sightly but increasingly antiquated Moguls, Consolidations, Ten-Wheelers and Atlantics throughout most of the road's operations in steam.

A first-class road that did not indulge in a fair-sized roster of 4-6-2 and 2-8-2 wheel arrangements was almost unheard of since the utilization of the two-wheel groups by the U.S.R.A. of World War I. Not until the advent of the high-speed overnight redballs in the 1930s did the road's management see fit to change its motive power, and then the Cotton Belt stepped into the age of the 4-8-4 with 20 beautifully designed machines, half from the Baldwin Locomotive Works and half from the company's own shops at Pine Bluff, Ark.

The pressure of World War II traffic forced the road to purchase yet another wheel arrangement that had long since found favor with first-class carriers, the 4-8-2 Mountain type. Cotton Belt bought secondhand units from both the Rock Island and the Florida East Coast, those from the latter being used almost exclusively in passenger service. (—*R. S. Plummer)*

Reminiscent of freight power on the Cotton Belt for nearly 50 years, a double-header of old stand-bys, 2-8-0 No. 754 and 2-6-0 No. 334, wheel a second section of the *Blue Streak Fast Freight* through the Dallas Union Terminal switchwork in 1948. (*—R. S. Plummer*)

At left Secondhand power at home. A former Rock Island 4-8-2, now Cotton Belt No. 682, gets a wheel on southbound tonnage on leased Missouri Pacific rails south of Dupo, Ill., while No. 6, the *Morning Star* — with as varied a selection of equipment as possible in such an abbreviated consist: an outside-framed fish-belly baggage car, two à la New Haven styled coaches and a heavyweight buffet-lounge-observation — rolls out of Dallas behind an ex-Florida East Coast 4-8-2.

Both groups of secondhand power were little altered from their original appearance, since the Cotton Belt contented itself with adding only chrome-plated engine numerals to the sand domes on each, as was the general practice. (—*Upper, William K. Barham; Lower, R. S. Plummer*)

Glistening in a brand-new coat of red enamel, Midland Valley caboose No. 61 is the very archetype of crummies bringing up the rear of many a steam-powered freight in years gone by, a far cry from extended-vision cupolas, electric lights, gas heaters and reflective paint in lieu of bona fide oil-fed markers. As the freshly stenciled reporting marks on the vertical planking show, the date of this paint job is October, 1936. (—*R. S. Plummer*)

Chromed cylinder heads, capped stack, blue-and-red company emblems on air-pump shields, striping on sand domes à la Frisco and 73-inch boxpok drivers — where have you been, you beautiful thing you!

The author is firmly convinced that some of the most beautifully maintained and aesthetically tasteful steam power in the nation rolled on the rails of the Texas and Pacific Railway. Unfortunately, as was often the case with such systems far from the centers of population, the aesthetic merits of the carrier's roster received little in the way of its "just dues" in print. Then witness, if you will, the appealing qualities of 4-8-2 No. 908 as it stretches out the 15-car consist of No. 8, the *Westerner*, on the Trinity River Bridge eastbound out of Dallas in 1948.

The inauguration of the blue-and-white *Texas Eagles*, operated jointly with the controlling Missouri Pacific Lines, created an even more glittering array of steam power. Although the streamlined consist of the *Eagle* itself was drawn by diesel power, there frequently were extra sections to contend with, plus a number of connections fanning out to various destinations on the system, all painted in the same light blue and off white with aluminum trim. An ordinary, black-painted steamer was not enough for this colorful varnish, and in true Texas fashion various units of the steam roster received matching paint schemes. (—R. S. Plummer)

Big, Elesco-browed Mountain No. 902 glitters in the morning light on the Texarkana enginehouse tracks, resplendent in a finery that includes a light-blue boiler jacket, cab and tender sides with a broad stripe of silver-bordered white, chromed cylinder covers, white-trimmed driver and lead-truck wheel rims, and company insignia in red and blue on air-compressor shields and mounted on the heater

itself. All in all No. 902 presents a startling yet tasteful bit of grandeur.

In the photo below, light Pacific No. 710 shines with the same impeccable decor, having only just emerged from the paint bay at the Marshall, Tex., shops in 1949. (*—both, R. S. Plummer*)

What the keystone number plate and horizontally slatted pilot were to the Pennsylvania; what double compressors on smokebox front and low-mounted headlight were to the Great Northern; or what the long, pointed pilot and extended stack were to the Santa Fe; so too were the flat-shielded double air compressors on pilot beam and the heavy-browed Elesco feedwater heater out front a trademark of the Texas and Pacific, and the standard-bearers of this line were the T.&P.'s 70 "I" class Lima-built 2-10-4s. *The* motive power on the T.&P. since their introduction in 1925, they possessed the most pleasingly impressive head-end countenance. Although a number of the group were counterbalanced for 60 an hour speeds and fitted with steam and signal hoses for passenger service, admirers of the type remember them best at the head end of that revenue-maker for the T.&P. — not to mention other southwestern haulers — the solid train of oil tanks. A virtual lifesaver for the nation during World War II, and a necessity for several years thereafter, those long strings of grimy-domed cylinders were dispatched with the greatest urgency, empty or full, as the war machines of the Allied armies desperately needed fuel. Until the advent of the big pipelines and ocean supertankers, the redball-carded oil trains rolling out of Oklahoma and Texas were frequent and fast. The T.&P. hauled its share, and hauled most of them behind the 600s.

Class I 2-10-4 No. 662, with that famous T.&P. look, faces the rising sun as it charges across the Trinity River Bridge near Dallas with a 75-car tank-train extra.

(—*R. S. Plummer*)

Don't let those empty yards fool you. Texas type No. 638 is the last of four tank-train extras thundering out of the Mineola, Tex., assembling yards in rapid succession. The crossover rails are ringing with the pounding of thousands of steel wheels picking up speed, and extra east No. 638 will only add to the bedlam as the pipe-laden monster accelerates rapidly onto the main. (—R. S. Plummer)

THE FRISCO LINE

To connoisseurs and aficionados of the age of steam, mere mention of the Frisco name means visions of Russian blue boiler jackets, distinctive gold-striped panels on tender and cab with a peculiar fretted motif at the corners, polished brass bells with gaping red mouths, chromed cylinder heads and immaculately shined running gear. All that was typical of this southwestern carrier whose motive power was — with the exception of a few fortunate buffs — largely "undiscovered" by photographers until the waning years of steam. For the most part a ridge runner of a railroad, with many of its route miles virtually hidden in the Ozark hills of Missouri, Arkansas and Alabama, it is unfortunate that this portion of the road's operations went unrecorded on film. However, photographers of merit were present and active at some of the road's major terminals and facilities to preserve the gallant grandeur of a railroad to which spit and polish was as important as fuel and water. Preston George of Oklahoma City did the honors at his end, while to the north in the St. Louis area the renowned team of William Barham and the late Ivan Oaks swore unfailing loyalty to the Frisco, aided immeasurably by Walt Schaffner and "Tex" Prusia, both gentlemen of patience and experience in collecting and preserving rare gems such as these.

The Frisco was never more deserving of devotion than in the years of the writer's youth, when the hours were spent in wide-eyed rapture alongside the engine leads at the Fyler Avenue engine terminal in west St. Louis as the Russian-blue-jacketed beauties were given last-minute rubdowns before their crews backed down to the Union Station platforms some six miles distant. There were high-domed and gilt-sided 1500 series Pacifics, all aglow in the late evening light, or robust Northerns both in blue-and-white passenger livery and in freight-only black with the speedy-looking "Frisco Faster Freight" red-wing emblem on the tender sides. Heaven was nigh when one of the understanding engine wipers thrust forward a fistful of waste, suggesting that the chromed cylinder heads needed polishing. Never did a cylinder head gleam as did those that night. Forgotten was the pants polishing that would be received upon arriving home with evidence of the joyous activities visible in stained trousers and shirt.

In the early years of World War II the parade west each evening was virtually endless: the *Texas Special* and *Meteor* were swollen to three and four sections each, running only minutes apart; all the while Scullin-drivered Pacifics and rawboned Northerns on the yard leads waited impatiently to follow the varnish hauls up the grade into the darkening dusk.

This was the Frisco! Polished cylinder heads and rod motion, gleaming brass bell, red-painted number plate with white trim, graphite smokebox and well-rubbed boiler jacket. No. 1519 stirs the overhead telltales as it sweeps past the St. Louis freight yards with the Texas-bound *Bluebonnet* in 1940. All that was dear to her admirers is embodied in this scene of the Frisco's trademark in steam at work. (*—Walter Schaffner*)

Recognizably and justifiably the Beau Brummells of the Frisco steam roster, the 1500 series Mountains had to give a share of their glory to their counterpart in freight service, the 4100 series big-boilered Mikados. Counterparts they were, too, having been constructed at the same time by the Baldwin Locomotive Works, with as many interchangeable parts as possible between the two classes of power, even to boilers, cabs and tenders. The result was entirely satisfactory, as demonstrated here by the immaculately maintained and well-proportioned top number of the group, No. 4164, pouring on the sand and steam while striding uphill near Stroud, Okla., in 1946 with a 35-car westbound redball. (*—Preston George*)

Delighting in their success at converting aging pre-World War I 4-6-2s and 2-10-2s into high-horsepower Hudsons and Mountain types in the late 1930s, the Frisco shops at Springfield, Mo., decided to go themselves one better and, following the fad of the times, stream-styled a member of the already aesthetically proven 1500 series 4-8-2s. In terms of design improvement the result was debatable. As was always the case with a one-of-a-kind, the distinctively garbed unit was indeed a rare item in glaring contrast to a roster of generally consistent appearance, but the effect was somehow unsatisfying. A generous use of stainless steel skirting edged with red enhanced the already tasteful design, but the large smokebox door and apron of sheet metal below it just didn't seem appropriate. The chosen victim of this venture, No. 1503, here poses on the inbound engine leads at St. Louis. (*—Robert J. Foster*)

Out on the main No. 1503 ignores the photographer's plea for a plume of smoke to accentuate its passing but nevertheless cuts a fine figure against the limestone bluffs at Pacific, Mo., with the eastbound *Bluebonnet*. (*—C. E. Prusia*)

Above Flying green at the smokebox and red on the tender, a big, burly, rawboned 4-8-4, No. 4511, slams past Southeastern Jct. and straight into the 2% grade out of the St. Louis yards with third No. 37, the *Oklahoma-Texas Fast Freight*. Despite the austerity of the war years 1942-43, during which these big Baldwins were built, the management's flare for the different had to be accommodated, resulting in the famous flying red wing and "Frisco Faster Freight" emblem on the tender sides. (—*William K. Barham*)

An equal amount of fireworks frames the approach of a less flamboyantly attired 4-8-2 on the page opposite, above, as company-built No. 4400, with trailing truck booster cut in to aid acceleration, departs Pacific, Mo., with the St. Louis-bound *Texas Special*. (—*R. S. Plummer*)

Below right In a more tranquil rendering at the opposite end of the carrier's network a considerably smaller member of the work force waits while the baggage handler stuffs a converted U. S. Army troop sleeper with Railway Express. The abbreviated consist is being readied for its final departure on June 30, 1951, from Vernon, Tex., for the all-day run to Enid, Okla. (—*J. T. McNamara*)

As amazing as the metamorphosis of the creeping caterpillar into a graceful, winged butterfly was the change wrought by the Frisco's Springfield shops in the rebuilding of 34 World War I drag-era 2-10-2s into two separate classes of good-looking high-horsepower 4-8-2s in 1936 and 1939. A generous sand dome atop a robust boiler, riding on 70-inch disc drivers specifically designed for the rebuilds by the Scullin Steel Company (whence the name was derived), topped off with those distinctive Frisco trademarks — the centered, visored headlight and the red-painted "coonskin" number plate — all combined to create a pièce de résistance in high-horsepower locomotives. That such a work of art could be reincarnated from the likes of 2-10-2 No. 50, pictured here in repose at Springfield, Mo., in its own heyday of drag-freight hauls, is a tribute to the company shops.

The very first of these rebuilds, No. 4300, rattles the shades and greets the dawn with a thunderous crack of exhaust at Pacific, Mo., as it gets under way with a westbound freight after a stop for water on November 15, 1937. (—Ivan Oaks)

A vignette of wintry railroading on a single-track line in the Ozarks. The eastbound peddler freight has gone in the siding at St. James, Mo., and waits patiently while a member of the rear-end crew eyes the photographer warily. Then the full crew waits on the platform to witness the duly scheduled meet with a westbound extra, and finally to receive a highball and a message, which only members of the railroad fraternity can interpret, from the hind-end crew as the cabooses pass in the quiet, white scene. (—Wayne Leeman)

213

A STUDY IN ILLINOIS CENTRAL MOUNTAINS

Steam action at its finest. Captured here by the camera of Walter Peters is all that goes with the drama and violence of a steam-driven train making time in the once traditional manner. A landmark in steam locomotive design, one of the Illinois Central's own company-built Mountain types is turning coal into smoke and steam, raising the dust from the roadbed and without a doubt shaking the floor of the tower at Tuscola, Ill. In a second those whirling drivers will smash across the gaps in the steel diamond and our ears will be deafened by the unceasing wham, wham, wham as hundreds of steel wheels pound unmercifully at the rail heads. How can any material withstand such an onslaught! While we are still drugged by such fury, the caboose will make the leap and the whole will fade in a cloud of dust, leaving our blood pressure to return slowly to normal. (*—Walter Peters*)

Further downstate in his native Illinois, photographer Peters does it again, another memorable scene from the years of steam. What could be more nostalgic than the station agent waving a highball to the hogger of a fast moving redball, as depicted so perfectly here by big-tank Illinois Central Mountain type No. 2613 pounding the single track north with a St. Louis-Chicago hotshot, circa 1950. (—*Walter Peters*)

No cab forward or hundred-car redball this, but as rare
a find as possible on Espee rails in 1949. A truly authentic 4-8-0 Twelve-Wheeler, with a tapered side main rod,
piping aplenty and a steam dome nearly equalling the
boiler diameter, waltzes merrily by the depot platform
at Eugene, Ore., with a lone boxcar and caboose, all
headed for the yards south of town to assemble a train
of log buggies for a day's work in the timber country.
(—Richard Wolf)

At right a big-nosed and big-domed 4-8-
No. 2919 awaits the day's chores at Eu
gene, Ore. A product of the Schenectad
Works in 1898, Twelve-Wheelers such a
this were synonymous with the Espee a
the turn of the century, as were the ca
forwards at the height of the road's stear
roster. (—Richard Wolf)

14.   What's New on the Southern Pacific?

Or more appropriately, what could be new on the S. P., as far as undiscovered material is concerned? Operating in that part of the United States blessed with more continual sunshine than any other region and with a roster of steam power encompassing nearly all wheel arrangements available, including its own original and justifiably famous cab forwards, the far-flung Southern Pacific Lines has enjoyed more photographic coverage accorded its trains and motive power than any other carrier. An author intending to proceed further into the subject is at a loss before he even starts. Thus it behooves one to reach deep into previously overlooked sources of material in an effort to ferret out some form of activity that has not basked in the glare of the stage lights, as indeed has the bulk of the Espee's operations.

Since most of the Southern Pacific's equipment and operations were concentrated within the state of California, where appropriately enough the same density of population has spawned a greater number of photographers than in other states, it is understandable that the most rarely observed operations should exist at the far-flung extremities of the Espee system. The logging operations of Oregon and the bayou branches of the Texas and New Orleans lines thus come in for their share of the limelight on the following pages, as donated by Dick Wolf and Johnnie Gray, of Kansas City and Little Rock, respectively. Now that these photographs have been brought to light, what else is new on the S. P.?

Fresh timber chained and pyramided atop its train of log buggies, Twelve-Wheeler No. 2952 makes its way cautiously through a rustic setting near Coquille, Ore., en route to Coos Bay, where its load of future two-by-fours will be dumped into the storage pond of the Coos Bay Lumber Company. (—Richard Wolf)

Cab forward in abbreviated form. Away at the other end of the far-flung system — in Houston, Tex., to be exact — a hostler's helper uses arms and legs to force water into the topside bunker of 0-6-0 tanker No. 3230 and waters down the surrounding area in the act. Used principally to shuffle dead motive power from shop to enginehouse or for a change in roundhouse stalls, tank engines such as this were not a favorite subject with most photographers. Resigned to a life almost entirely confined to a particular roundhouse and the nearest fueling facility, such saddle tankers were akin to a recalcitrant and nocturnal tortoise in their habits. (—R. S. Plummer)

Shades of New England! Deep in the tall timber of central Oregon 2-8-0 No. 2506 pops tender-first out of an authentic covered bridge. The bridge spans the Mohawk River, a name also somewhat removed from its natural habitat, and No. 2506 is easing across the aged structure with an early-morning local on the Springfield-to-Marcola branch. Since no turning facilities existed at Marcola, this rearward operation was the accepted practice on the uprun, while the return trip was performed in a more orthodox manner. (—Richard Wolf)

Not all Espee 4-8-0s whiled away their working hours hauling log buggies in Oregon. Fatsoes like No. 2914, shown here wheeling company gondolas near Connors, Calif., treated California fans to one of the rarest of American wheel arrangements in smoky action. (—Donald Duke)

Move south from Oregon into California and the inevitable happens, at least it did in steam days: a flash of red, orange and glossy black adds splendor to the beauty of the Golden State in the form of the S.P.'s never-to-be-forgotten *Daylight* streamliner. Powered by the finest of all attempts at steam stream-styling, Lima-built GS class 4-8-4s, the daily passage of these trains on the Los Angeles-San Francisco haul was spellbinding.

What's new about another in the seemingly endless photographic record of this fine train? Nothing really, except that in this splendid view by Richard Kindig all that was symbolic of this train is captured at its best: a mighty 4-8-4 polished and gleaming; tapered main rod spinning four pairs of 80-inch boxpok drivers at an 80-an-hour gait; smoke and steam hard against an early-morning sky; and the unbroken harmony of 13 fluted-side and revenue-loaded cars rolling smoothly behind. A stirring scene at Chatsworth, Calif., in October, 1941.

Something old, something new
— and definitely not blue, but solid
black on the profit ledger —
a trainload of fresh perishables
is hurried toward eastern appetites
behind an old man of the Espee.
The last of four redballs out of
California, this string of freshly
iced P.F.E. "reefers" is rolling over
the primeval landscape near
Sentinel, Ariz., behind a Santa Fe
type (an ugly word in this
instance), one of 120 such engines
that were the backbone of S.P.
desert railroading in this year of
1939. (—*Donald Duke Collection*)

223

Moving the finished products that resulted from the logging expeditions of the 4-8-0s in Oregon fell chore to that famous tribe of singular cab forwards, which were an offspring, years removed, of the fat-boilered Twelve-Wheelers themselves. The cab forwards here are not new to the printed page, but the line over which they are operating is. No Donner Pass or Tehachapi with towering peaks to point up the mass of the locomotive, these bleak and desolate surroundings are encountered in moving lumber products from Oregon to the east-west main line at Fernley, Nev. Fifty-foot boxcars and flatcars loaded high with boards are the traffic, and cab forwards in multiples are needed to move them, for however flat and unassuming the terrain appears, formidable grades abound on the Alturas cutoff (often referred to as "the Modoc").

Hank Griffiths, famous for his photography on the Union Pacific's Blue Mountain grade, penetrated this desert fastness at sunrise to make these memorable recordings of a pair of A.C.'s urging an even hundred loads of lumber south out of Likely, Calif., on the Modoc. A study in stark black and white like this would normally be impossible at such an early hour, except in the western desert air. Elsewhere haze and damp night mists would cut off the sun's first rays and spoil the clarity and brilliance of these photographs.

Powered by yet another of the famous *Daylight* design 4-8-4s, only two digits removed from the one shown previously, No. 4437 sails through Chatsworth at 60 an hour with 27 cars of *CME*, a San Francisco-Los Angeles overnight merchandise train running on a schedule only slightly slower than the famed *Daylight* itself. (—*Richard Kindig*)

Broomsticks and smoke plumes. The leasing of spare motive power to bolster the overworked roster of a wholly owned subsidiary was nothing new in railroad operations, but aesthetically the combination was something else! Steeple-cab motors of the normally all-electric Pacific Electric received an assist from the parent Espee's steam power during a welcome rush of traffic in late 1945. Ten-Wheeler No. 2283 coats the catenary with oil soot while motor No. 1626 hums angrily behind, as together they hustle a mixed-consist extra through Wilmar, Calif. Twenty-eight cars to the rear 2-8-0 No. 2701 pushes for good measure. (—*William K. Barham*)

A rare treat for the photographer seeking the unusual among the remnants of S.P. steam in 1951 was 2-6-6-2 No. 3930 pounding through Bassett, Calif., with a lengthy drag and a clean stack, much to the annoyance of that same photographer. The grimy old mauler came to the Espee from the Verde Tunnel and Smelter Railway and hung around to the last on the carrier's roster of motive power. (—*William K. Barham*)

Twisting and turning at the whim of nature, the *San Joaquin Daylight* rolls ponderously through Soledad Pass to the beat of 4-8-4 road engine No. 4421 and helper No. 4352. In this 1944 scene the MT-4 class Mountain type helper displays the later trademarks of Espee passenger power: chromed cylinder heads, white-edged running boards, polished boiler, bolted-on cabside numerals and a line of neat, roman characters spelling out the carrier's name on the tender — a far cry from the yardstick-high lettering and corrugated pilots that were a Southern Pacific trademark in 1940. (*—William K. Barham*)

229

On the flat, grassy Louisiana marshes, where a rise of a few feet means the difference between dry and wet firmament, a 2-8-2 and a 2-8-0 are easing out on the main iron with a westbound freight after taking the siding to allow the division's main varnish run — designated appropriately enough, No. 1 — to pass at speed.

The rear brakeman, having taken advantage of the stop to walk forward and inspect the train, waits now for the string of gondolas and high cars to clear the switch so that, as his counterpart is doing in the accompanying shot of another Texas and New Orleans run, he may close and lock the switch in one deft movement and sprint for the caboose steps before the hogger, who judges the distance by car lengths, decides he is in the clear and widens on the throttle. Should either the hogger's judgment be premature or the brakie's sprint inadequate, it would be his crewmate's duty to pull the air and stop the train, always certain to rile both the head-end crew and the dispatcher. (—*Johnnie Gray*)

Indicative of the Espee power one generally saw in motion is this 4-8-2, No. 4302, helping a GS-4 Northern type, running five hours late and hitting the grade at Beaumont Hill, Calif., with the 17 heavyweight cars of the *Argonaut* in 1948. (*—Donald Duke*)

Although photographers and railfans still cherish the "burning-of-Rome" smoke effects, the volcanic eruption from the stacks of these veteran Espee freight maulers would today create pandemonium among the anti-pollutionists. Great gobs of the thick, black stuff were commonplace during S.P. steam operations, and ironically it was the lower echelons of power that provided the greatest pillars, as demonstrated by Mogul No. 1751, hogging the show with a sky-blackener near Nicklin, Calif., or Consolidations Nos. 2338 and 2350, whose head-end crews are hanging from the cab windows grabbing for air as they exit a tunnel near Searles Junction, Calif., under a twin canopy that may be likened unto Mt. Etna at the height of eruption. (—Donald Duke)

233

The introduction of the Mogul to the American railroad scene during the last decades of the 1800s was a marked improvement over the 4-4-0 American then enjoying a monopoly as the standard motive power throughout the country. The Mogul won immediate acceptance as a heavy-freight hauler, usually doubling the tonnage that had been pulled by its ancestor, the 4-4-0. However, after the years just past, with super articulateds hauling 100-car drags and tonnage readings in the thousands, it seems ridiculous and even a bit humorous to relate that the 2-6-0 wheel arrangement was accorded the title "Mogul" because of its ability to move high-tonnage trains.

During World War I, with the advent of the drag-era and its veritable dinosaurs of steam locomotives, the 2-6-0 fell into disfavor and was usually scrapped or moved to the innumerable branch lines with their light rail and light loads. By the end of World War II one would be hard put to find the ancient and quaint wheel arrangement on any but a few backwoods short-

line carriers or the seemingly forgotten segments of the large systems. And yet on the Espee, right up until the visible end of steam, the indomitable Moguls could still be found thundering the main iron with a respectable cut of tonnage or as lead helper engine on the most prestigious varnish hauls. The far flung carrier had many Moguls, in a variety of sizes, spread throughout the system. No. 506, a Mogul of generous proportions, wheels a fair-sized mixed run near the Texas-Louisiana state line while on the opposing run on another day a low-slung and more antiquated No. 424 smokes up the girders of a swing bridge over one of the area's many irrigation canals. (—Johnnie Gray)

Sporting the familiar whaleback tender of S.P. fame, No. 1758 waits to hustle an extra out of Eugene, Ore. All of this in the twilight of steam operations on the mighty Southern Pacific Lines. (—Richard Wolf)

234

235

Over and under condensed into one view. Our intrepid cameraman has now stationed himself dead-center in front of an eastbound time freight curving out of the tunnel behind a big Mike which is about to set foot ponderously on the deck of the river crossing. The bridge structure is certainly a relic of the steam era, as evidenced by its mass of iron struts, bracing and the like. This is a horizontal swing bridge which must open frequently to allow tows to pass underneath, and both the bridge and the track-work are controlled from an operator's shanty perched precariously in the ironwork directly overhead. (—Johnnie Gray)

15. *Over and Under at Hannibal, Missouri*

Once, a photographer could pleasurably spend several busy hours at one of those little hot spots of railroading tucked away into some inconspicuous accident of topography. These idyllic places were once numerous throughout the United States; a junction hidden in the lee of a bluff, a crossing of two high-speed mains lying bare on the prairie flatlands, or an interchange point between a ravine-wandering short line and the curving, heavy-duty double-track main of a coal hauler in the deep Allegheny canyons. They were known only to the local populace, if there was one, and to the railroad crews who enlivened their sheltered existence at frequent intervals. It is unfortunate that many such operations went unrecorded throughout the years of the steam locomotive, for although in part they may well have survived into today's diesel-oriented railroading, with its automated methods of signaling and train handling, there was a certain aura about such locations that only the clanking outside motion of a steam locomotive could bring out.

One such haven of activity fortunately preserved on film while steam power yet pounded the rail joints is the intersection of the Burlington's single-track north-south route, from St. Louis to the main line at Burlington, Iowa, with the single-track iron of the Wabash Railroad's busy freight division, reaching from the Decatur, Illinois, division point to Kansas City, Missouri.

The distinguishing feature of the whole location is the manner in which the Wabash approaches the intersection with the Burlington. It is here that the Wabash bridges the wide Mississippi River only to find itself square against the towering limestone bluffs that parallel Ole Man River for hundreds of miles in either direction. This creates the second distinguishing feature of the intersection, for the only alternative left to the original construction engineers was an immediate tunnel through to a narrow ravine on the opposite side of the bluff. As if the bridge approach and pier, plus the railroad diamond and tunnel entrance, were not enough to locate on a few feet of river ledge, a public automobile road has intruded between the tunnel entrance and railroad crossing, with protective gates at that! All in all, a very tempting treat for the railroad photographer with a little imagination.

Enter such a cameraman, while smoke still wafts from the tunnel portal. Johnnie Gray of Little Rock, presently an Arkansas State Highway Department staff photographer, was one of those admirers of both steam and diesel who felt no compulsion to excel in any one style of railroad photography but chose instead to photograph trains as he saw them, from any angle, in any location, with plenty of natural habitat for a setting. Once frowned upon by the purists, his photographs and others like them are today considered rare gems not only because they exhibit a medium of transport now considerably altered but also for their unusual views of the locomotive, the train and the lineside panorama. His views of the trackwork itself, as shown in the accompanying photographs, depict both crossings and switch rodding, and are valuable aids for modelers seeking to reconstruct the railroad world of yesteryear in miniature.

It may have been tight quarters for big-boilered Mikado No. 2713 inside that bore, but it will be an even tighter squeeze for the photographer, who had best melt into that rock-walled cut while the 60-odd-car freight rumbles through westbound at Hannibal, Mo. (—*Johnnie Gray*)

Having just snared a 19 order from the operator's hoop, the rear-end brakeman retreats into his red-painted crummy as the big 2-8-2 hustles the freight across the bridge and out onto the Illinois prairies. (—*Johnnie Gray*)

With little warning 0-6-0 No. 563 pops out of the tunnel bore, smoking and hissing, bent on several switching chores across the river. Needless to say, this is a blind crossing! (—*Johnnie Gray*)

Wabash No. 2275 has left the river crossing well behind and is working up speed on the Mississippi river bottoms for a run at the short but steep climb to the top of the bluffs just ahead. No. 2275 is one of the two heavy Mikado designs that regularly pounded the trackwork at the Hannibal crossing.

Although flat-faced and homely, the Burlington's graphited, extended-smokebox 2-8-2s did possess a certain appeal of their own. Perhaps it was nostalgia, since for many midwesterners the first encounter with a steam locomotive included the muffled exhaust and low, moaning whistle of a "Q" Mike puttering about the grain elevators and trackside spurs of their home town; wherever one lived in the granger states, the Burlington invariably poked its rails into the center of things. No. 5328 is "woofing" it up along the riverbank well to the north of Hannibal with a long string of empties. (*—Charles Ost*)

As much a part of the Old South as a mint julep in the evening and a dab of grits in the morning, a beautifully painted and polished sylvan green Southern Railway 4-6-2 glides flawlessly through the lush green of the August countryside near Bon Air, Va., in 1948 with the abbreviated and polished dark-green consist of accommodation run No. 7. A stylish individuality in motive power and a rural charm in passenger hauls graced the backwoods rails of the Southern and its Dixie cousins. (—August A. Thieme, Jr.)

16. Southern Hospitality, or "Keep off the right of way"

The South was once endowed with surely the quaintest and most appealing collection of rural short-line railroads in America, many of whose wanderings have been poetically and humorously described in the greatest work of all time on this American institution, *Mixed Train Daily* by the renowned Lucius Beebe. The railroad systems of the South, whether short or long, were said to have a friendliness and rural charm one would be hard put to find elsewhere. Green and gold-striped motive power, Saluda grade, short but frequent trains, rural backgrounds and that powerful ingredient, hospitality, all served as incentive for this writer to wander across the Mason-Dixon line into the Deep South for a taste of it all.

This first taste was garnished by Mother Nature, who welcomed this itinerant photographer and a fellow companion into the hills of Tennessee with a fiery display of lightning and shrouds of rain, which made driving on the mountainous roads at night a not-too-pleasurable experience. Since financial funds in the early days of such wanderings were slim and usually stretched beyond capacity, we were wont to live off the lean of the land, so to speak. Thus it behooved us to carry sufficient sleeping arrangements of our own, and in practice these consisted of a pair of folding cots which were opened up at the proper time in some remote rural corner where disturbances would be at a minimum. Thereupon at the first lessening of the tiresome drenching we chose what in the dark and gloom appeared to be a rural road of little consequence and turned down it. Sleeping quarters were immediately effected and the first night of rest in Dixie was at hand.

It was not to be a night without interruption, however, for after a few hours of sound slumber we were prodded into wakefulness to find the long arm of the obviously local law at our side, inquiring as to our recumbency in this locale. After a sleepy-voiced explanation of the storm, darkened roads and the need for rest in an unknown area, the sheriff's sympathy was won and, in a slow southern drawl this author shall never forget, we were told, "Sahleep on then fellas, sahleep on." And we did. At the first gray light of dawn, as we rolled out of our opulent quarters, the reason for the law's concern was obvious: in the dark and rain we had unknowingly driven down the service road and into the middle of the Johnson City sports stadium! We departed as quickly and as inconspicuously as possible before gendarmes of less sympathy appeared on the scene.

Our joy in the leniency of the law was to be short-lived, however, for a few days later, while under the hypnotic spell cast by the lovable U.S.R.A. power of the Western of Alabama, the Atlanta and West Point and the Georgia Line, assembled in quantities around the Atlanta engine terminal, we were again accosted by the long arm of the railroad law and, instead of being invited to sleep on, were told in no less than harsh terms to "git!" Still chafing under this infraction of the much-expected southern hospitality as we departed Atlanta, we decided perhaps we would be more fortunate if we confined our activities to smaller engine terminals, and we immediately proceeded to Camak Junction on the Georgia Railroad. No sooner had we set foot upon the premises and peered into the haze of summer heat in hopes of seeing a live steamer than a burly individual, quite reminiscent of the stories of midnight kangaroo courts, descended upon us and in a voice we had decided reeked with true southern hospitality invited us to leave the area at once or "git shot at." We left.

With loud lamentations and denunciations of the now much-overrated and obviously farcical southern hospitality, we rolled into the sleepy-streeted town of Milledgeville, Georgia, where we decided that a meal of sorts might cool the fires of resentment now burning so furiously. Little choice was immediately available, since only one greasy spoon, as we were wont to call the eating establishments of the road, existed in this one-dog community. We entered and ordered what might be the most neutral of the menu's offerings. The rather rotund and motherly waitress, who also doubled as cook, dishwasher and owner, made inquiry as to our residence, neither of us possessing the typical southern drawl needed to pass as a native. Upon learning of our neo-Yankee origins she inquired rather innocently as to our thoughts on southern hospitality. Oh, poor innocent victim of circumstance that she was, our complaints and sufferings fell upon her ears without mercy. Undaunted she was, though, and retiring to the confines of the kitchen she vowed that no young gentlemen down to see Georgia would return home with thoughts anything other than pleasurable. Thus, to our complete surprise, as we rose to take leave, this emissary of good will presented us with a basket of fried chicken, corn on the cob, hush-puppies and a jug of cold water to wash this repast down. We thanked her profusely and vowed that southern hospitality did indeed exist!

Perhaps the key to the expected hospitality of the South was the identifying drawl that is as much a trademark to the South as were the once eye-appealing green-and-gold PS-4s of the Southern. Obviously Frank Ardrey of Birmingham, Alabama, possessed the needed patois, since credit for much of the photographic record of the South's steam power in action as presented here goes to this gentleman, who generously offered his fine collection and again proved that southern hospitality still exists.

Johnson City, Tenn., was not only good for a night's rest but ech to the glorious thunder of Clinchfield Mallets going their mountai way. A ridge-leaping railway that tries to be a north-south br route in a land where the topography insists on east-west travel, Clinchfield is endowed with heavy grades, many long, high s trestles, and tunnels and curves, all demanding the use of M articulated power. Station names like Switzerland, Tenn., indi the skills needed to photograph adequately the road's motive po at work: mountain climbing was almost a necessity.

Challenger type No. 661 is climbing to Ridge, Tenn., shoulderin₈ cars of southbound extra, while older Mallets of U.S.R.A. vintage ₅ ply the booster power needed to gain the Blue Ridge heights. (—Ro Collins)

Famed Sherman Hill is synonymous with Union Pacific, and the Rio Grande has its Tennessee Pass, while to the east Horseshoe Curve and the Pennsylvania are one. Appropriately enough, the land below the Mason-Dixon line did not lack such thunderous spectacles of men, machines and nature at odds; the South's most famous contribution to the list of sand-polished rails and straining rods was the Southern and its fabled Saluda Grade. Saluda, situated almost midway between Spartanburg, S.C., and Asheville, N.C., is a virtual stepladder up the Blue Ridge.

Saluda is a bare nine miles in length, but is the steepest main-line, standard-gauge grade in the United States, ranging from 3.7 to 4.7%. It took the biggest of Southern steam power, and in multiples at that, to lift tonnage into the "city in the clouds." Saluda was all that a mountain grade should be in the years of steam: slow-paced, straining stack exhausts; low drivers crunc ing sand into a fine powdery mist; helpers fore and aft pulli and pushing through deep cuts and over high bridges, with t added attraction of steeply inclined safety tracks to catch erra runaways on the steep downgrade.

In this vibrant scene of steam on Saluda in 1948, a brace of b boilered 2-10-2s are clawing for momentum in an almost fut attempt to get a run on the steepest part of the grade after stop at the Melrose coal chute to fill the tender bunkers. A sca 30 cars back, the smoke of the helper is visible as No. 50 puts its muscle to the charge. Melrose is at the bottom of t 4.7% and even as the helper passes the camera lens all thr locomotives are down on their hands and knees. (—*Frank Ardre*

Hot and panting mightily from a lusty battle with the Blue Ridge, Southern green-and-gold 4-8-2 No. 1491 pauses at Old Fort, N.C., to gulp a tank of water and blow her top, figuratively speaking, as safety pops and stack exhaust respond to the fireboy's readiness for the grades just ahead. (*—Dale Roberts*)

Of special interest to admirers of Southern steam was the archaic and picturesque frame and brick enginehouse at Selma, Ala. Dating back to antebellum days, its louvered smoke jacks, arched doorways and steeply tilted roof housed an endearing collection of motive power. Its guests were small and delicately balanced wheel arrangements operating on a multitude of little-known branch lines into the piney woods of the Gulf Coast region.

On an early February morning in 1947 a proverbial Beau Brummell, apple green and gold-trimmed Ten-Wheeler No. 949, warms up on the appropriately condensed turntable serving the house. Before the day becomes much brighter the high-domed and adorable pony will scurry south with the daily passenger train for Mobile. In a complementary pose, slender-boilered Consolidation No. 7 takes a ride on the light-of-load table before it follows the green-painted 949 south to Mobile. At the time of this photograph No. 7 had the distinction of being the only remaining one-digit locomotive on the Southern, a situation it enjoyed principally because of a restrictive weight limit on the Tombigbee River Bridge at Jackson, Ala. (—Frank Ardrey)

A mountain mauler at rest. The biggest steam power on the Southern Railway, or in the Deep South itself, true Mallet articulated No. 4057 poses for the photographer in front of the Birmingham, Ala., coal dock before being called forth again to do battle with the grades of the Great Smokies. Definitely an unwelcome guest at Selma house. (—*Frank Ardrey*)

The *South Wind* breezes through Dixieland behind U.S.R.A. look-alikes. A joint venture of the Pennsylvania, the Louisville and Nashville and the Atlantic Coast Line, the *South Wind* was a seasonal, all-coach Chicago-Florida vacationland train of Budd stainless-steel equipment. Except for the bullet-nosed K-4s normally assigned by the Pennsy to the Chicago-Louisville lap, the consist moved behind conventional U.S.R.A. 4-6-2s, as shown here. A.C.L. No. 1533, its white striping obscured by road grime, brings the streamlined consist into Montgomery, Ala., while the L.&N.'s No. 279 snakes the same consist out of the station throat for a fast run north to waiting Pennsy power at Louisville. (*—Frank Ardrey*)

CENTRAL OF GEORGIA

While one may gaze intently upon the scores of photographs and books that have been dedicated to railroads, it is the actual visual and personal acquaintance, developed through close association with a particular carrier, its operations and equipment, that forms a lasting and loyal memory for most of us. Such was the case with the Central of Georgia, which endeared itself to the author in many ways during several months of captivity within the United States Army, part of the time spent in the red hills around Ft. Benning. There the day's greatest joy was a Central of Georgia 4-8-4 rattling the aged barracks timbers at dawn, hauling the northbound and homeward bound *Seminole* on the main iron a few yards distant.

Although controlling interest in the line was vested in the Illinois Central's Chicago headquarters, little of any such influence could be found in the C. of G.'s motive power, where conventional round domes were the rule, and vertically stacked Elesco feedwater heaters did all but hide the stack from view. Red-and-white heralds on tender flanks and a generous use of white trim on running boards and driving-wheel rims were more in keeping with the Dixie style than the very utilitarian all-black garb of the parent road's motive power.

Central of Georgia No. 709, a 2-10-2 of obvious U.S.R.A. origin, arouses the late sleepers at Irondale, Ala., with an eastbound freight running under open safety valves.

The vertical, twin-stacked Elesco feedwater heater was not employed to any great extent by American locomotive builders, since most railroads preferred the more common horizontal-cylinder styles such as New York Central and the like. But Central of Georgia's Mountain type No. 488 displays this rare appliance with little pretense at concealment as it rolls into the junction at Weems, Ala., with the Birmingham-to-Columbus local No. 2. (*—Frank Ardrey*)

Although splendidly represented by such handsome specimens as the Nashville, Chattanooga and St. Louis' yellow jackets and the Atlantic Coast Line's white-striped Baldwins, the 4-8-4 was a relative rarity on the southern railroad scene. The C. of G. had the distinction of operating the third such group of locomotives in the Deep South. Designated Class K and essentially a C. of G. stylized version of the Southern Pacific's GS-2 minus skirting, the eight engines inherited many design characteristics from already existent C. of G. power, which resulted in a 4-8-4 that looked somewhat askew. What with its large smokebox door; narrow pressed-steel pilot; radiator and air filters protruding over the pilot beam; vertical Elesco heater; and a tender quite abbreviated and inappropriate for the size of the engine, and riding on four wheel trucks at that — the aesthetics were, in a word, questionable.

However, all of this was completely forgotten one night in 1949, during the return of a Columbus-to-Birmingham excursion, while 22 carloads of local revelers danced, sang

and downed gallons of beer, along with many a pound of catfish fried in the baggage cars, this steam-crazed writer wormed his way into the cab of a Class K, the second engine of a pair on the head end, and became more tipsy than any of the booze-filled revelers in the cars to the rear, as the pair of Northerns stack-talked and whistled their way over the undulating Alabama landscape under a full moon.

Appropriately posed against a stand of the jack pine for which the South is famous — or infamous as the case may be — No. 452 is at Weems, Ala., heading toward Birmingham with third No. 9, the *Seminole*. The *Seminole* was a maid-of-all-work passenger haul between Chicago and Jacksonville, Fla., and its strings of heavyweights were regularly assigned to an able Class K for forwarding over the Georgia and Alabama landscape.

Above right   K class No. 455 waits for the highball under the cathedral-like towers of the Birmingham Terminal station in June of 1948. (*—Frank Ardrey*)

254

Both hogger and charge appear properly attired and freshly scrubbed as together they wheel No. 38, the *Crescent*, out of Montgomery, Ala., for the run to Atlanta in this 1947 view. Pacific No. 190 on the head end and a companion-class engine, the Atlanta and West Point's No. 290, were regularly assigned this lap of the *Crescent's* New Orleans-New York journey. *(—Frank Ardrey)*

With rails flung from the Gulf to Chicago and west across Iowa, it is entirely possible to err in considering the Illinois Central a Dixie railroad. But one can hardly ignore the carrier's presence as it darts across Alabama to Birmingham and cuts a double swath the length of Mississippi while radiating branch lines across the state.

Trotter's Point, Miss., is the setting for this study of steam on both rails and the river, where in 1950 the Central's own *Pelican*, a true side-wheeler in the old tradition, bridged Ole Man River in a manner as picturesque and, alas, as obsolete as the steam locomotive itself. Plying the width of the river to the Arkansas shore, the wide-beam rarity not only ferried freight cars but carried on board a jaunty 2-8-0, with pumps on the pilot beam, to perform the loading and unloading chores. Smoke-spuming No. 726 arches out onto the approach dock after reaching into the *Pelican's* maw for a string of debarking loads.

The Gulf, Mobile and Ohio until it acquired the Alton Road in the late 1940s, operated in the areas associated with the first two words of its corporate title and thus was under the Dixie influence. Certainly its use of large headlights and lengthy pilots on motive power mostly of U.S.R.A. ancestry, a design which seemingly saturated the South, justifies placing the old G.M.&O. in the Dixie fold.

Mikado No. 461 holds to the main as the hogger widens on the throttle after getting a clear board at the Bixby, Ill., passing track with 62 steam-era cars headed for the road's then northernmost terminus at East St. Louis, Ill.

(—above, William K. Barham)
(—at right, Johnnie Gray)

Class O-1a Mike No. 4983 rattles the windows of the old frame tower at Mendota, Ill., as it clatters over the I.C. crossings with a local freight east. As of this writing the tower still stands, reportedly the only such structure remaining on the length of the Burlington's main line. It is a remnant of the host of guardian watchtowers from Chicago to Omaha that have all gone, almost fittingly, with the steam locomotives whose progress they guided.

17. Summer Idyll at Mendota, Illinois

        Some 83 miles west of Chicago, as the Burlington Route lies, is the railroad-junction town of Mendota, where the "Q's" main iron west crosses both the Illinois Central's freight line, from mid-Illinois to Madison, Wisconsin, and a wandering branch of the Milwaukee Road. With its antiquated, red-painted frame interlocking tower, guarding a multitude of switches, diamonds and derails through which a steady flow of traffic moves, what better place could there be to spend a summer evening in August of 1949 — especially after an arduous day in the concrete congestion of Chicago, futilely pursuing steam through crowded quarters and depressing backdrops, all under the baleful eyes of overly zealous railroad police and minor officials. The more dignified comings and goings of steam in a setting of rural platitudes, under a lowering sun of nearly endless intensity, was as soothing a medicine as could be found. Mendota is a world of its own, living apart from the encroaching internal-combustion oblivion and the dubious march of progress. Spend an hour at Mendota on a distant August evening, if you will.

Mendota was also an important fuel and water stop in the days of
steam power, and although the long arms of the coaling facility there
beckon invitingly, the crew of 0-5 Northern No. 5618 has decided
to ignore the invitation and keep a roll on the 100-odd cars of westbound freight.

A rare treat for us this evening, an Illinois Central Mikado, No. 2119, clatters over the crossing and then slips into the passing track with a southbound string of empty hoppers.

While the southbound extra's crew is seated at the local beanery, stoking the inner man, their meet is made with 2-8-2 No. 2131 and 86 loads of northbound coal. The big-cylindered Mike has a clear board for the "Q" diamond just ahead, and the hogger widens on the throttle in anticipation of his own meal stop, some miles distant.

The only discordant note of modern times to break steam's spell that idyllic summer evening was the muffled roar of three units of diesel power whisking the stainless-steel, multidomed *California Zephyr* into a setting sun that it would pursue all across the bountiful West to the ocean's edge, some 2,000 miles distant. Diesel or no, it seemed not unlike the *Queen Mary* passing Lands End for a destination half a world away.

Northern No. 5625, the Burlington's one experiment with the Franklin system of poppet valves, was not successful enough to warrant duplication but, judging from its resplendent condition, was still considered worthy of use. Here No. 5625 loafs effortlessly through the Mendota interlocking with an 80-car extra west. Several hours later in the dark of the night the author encountered this same locomotive, which had obviously spent the time setting out cars at some of the many in-between junctions, now racing through Wyanet, Ill., faster than any freight train he had ever witnessed. Were it not for the awe and fascination of the spectacle, absolute fear would have set in as the big Northern topped a rise and descended on the unsuspecting hamlet, while the highway flashers frantically spelled, "Danger, get away," and the local station agent balefully drawled, "He's got a roll on her tonight." And he certainly did: with whistle screaming, high cars rocking and pitching in protest, the mass of iron and wood literally exploded into view. Then it was gone, as flickering caboose markers disappeared into a cloud of dust and smoke. One could only stare after them in awe.

18. *Little Friends in the Backwoods*

They served as they were meant to serve, those little pikes of unballasted forty-pound rail and a single steam locomotive, little railroads where the vice-president loaded freight and sold a solitary ticket, where hand firing was the only way, and a mixed run daily except Sunday was the informal schedule. These little railroads of the backwoods were built to go where main lines and superhighways did not, and they served to connect such monsters of progress with a more remote and older world of shady four-corner communities.

These rural feeders of a pleasant yesteryear can trace their creation to the desire of every community, at some distant point in time, to be on the railroad, and when passed by in the great days of railroad construction as some must be, these backwoods towns persisted stubbornly toward their goal. Subscribed to with local funds, and with completion to some not-too-distant mainline connection a cause for a community celebration, each short line was delicately integrated into the region it traversed, its comings and goings the concern of all. The short-line railroad flourished in direct proportion to the life of a rural America, and the transition of the United States from an agricultural to an industrial nation inevitably spurred the decline of the little carriers.

As a happy hunting ground for the connoisseur of railroading, they reflected a tranquility in their operations quite different from the businesslike intent of big-time railroading. A railbuff bent upon ferreting out and witnessing a day's operation on an American short line in the thirties or forties, at a time when yet a respectable quantity of such remnants still existed, found himself in a world of individualism, self-sufficiency and a general informality of operations, spawning experiences and memories the likes of which were not to be had in any other medium of transport.

Consider the Kelly's Creek and Northwestern, a coal-hauling short line nearly seven miles long in deepest West Virginia. Connecting with the New York Central, now the Penn Central, at Cedar Grove, several miles east of Charleston, and extending back into the harsh ravines of this rugged land, the carrier was wont to perform its operations, almost shamefacedly, in the darker hours of the night, principally to pick up the loaded cars filled with coal in the day's operation of the hill-hugging mines. The author encountered this night train completely assembled, with a Civil War-period caboose and some twenty battered hopper cars, barred from interchange with any first-class common carrier. Very happily for this explorer, the pièce de résistance sat at the head of the assemblage, a squat-boilered Consolidation of questionable ancestry, appropriately designated No. 1, alternately sighing and popping off between the throbs of the single wheezing air compressor.

An introduction and an explanation of the author's desires was all it took to gain an invitation from the crew to spend the night in their carousings. In short order the rotund hoghead kicked off the air and horsed her over, and the hot-boilered Consolidation came to life. With cinders rattling on the galvanized tin roof of the company store and bouncing on the hoods of autos parked near-by at the local gin mill, which was doing a booming business at that hour of the evening, we barked out of town and into the darkness of the West Virginia night.

The gully grade was steep and our progress was slow as the rough-riding steamer jostled us around a curve and into an even narrower ravine, made thrice so by a seemingly endless row of grimy, gray-painted company homes, which thrust their monotonously identical front stoops within arm's reach of the cab window. Our pace was no more than a walk on the uphill climb, and arms were upraised in greeting as comments passed from the crew to onlookers taking their leisure on these same porch railings after a day in the mines. This first-time visitor was lulled into a sense of serenity, a feeling suddenly shattered as the tall, lanky head-end brakeman, who was riding the cab cushions, let out with a whoop and literally dived out the gangway on the opposite side of the cab. The reason for this action was soon apparent. On the porch of a home we were slowly approaching stood a rough-and-tumble character, straight out of the Hatfield-McCoy feud, who swore in no uncertain terms that we must stop so that he could blow that no-good so-and-so's brains out, emphasizing his demands by pointing the meanest-looking shotgun imaginable into our cab confines. This certainly wasn't part of the tranquility described in Lucius Beebe's *Mixed Train Daily!*

All the time there reposed on the same front stoop a young lady of Lulu Belle-like appearance, head lowered and obviously in a very family way. It was apparent that the fast-disappearing brakeman had figured in a romance of less than sincere intentions. It was only after the hogger and fireboy explained at length that the intended victim was not aboard that the irate would-be assassin withdrew his, by that time, cannon-sized firearm from the gangway and we moved on, all of us heaving a sigh of relief. At a safe distance further up the grade the cowering Romeo put in his appearance, only to receive a well-deserved cursing by the rest of the crew.

The remainder of the night's operations proceeded in a more or less orderly manner, setting out and picking up empties and loads from a score of dimly lit coal tipples, where miners' hats bobbed like fireflies on an August night as the ground-hugging coal jimmies emerged to dump their loads and then returned to the blackened catacombs of the earth. At least it was a normal night's run until the hogger, a short, and rather Humpty Dumpty-like man, became impatient waiting for a switch to be thrown and began to berate the fireboy and head brakie, who were both off in a nearby creek bed, their lanterns bobbing in the dark. In spite of the hoghead's demand that they get on with the switchwork, they both returned to the engine cab announcing that they had a present for the hogger, whereupon they deposited on his lap the biggest and slimiest frog this author had ever seen. With one wild whoop the hogger immediately disappeared out the cab window! He could not be coaxed back into the cab until he was reassured repeatedly that the creature had fallen through the floor openings and departed for elements more natural.

The newly risen sun had failed to dispel the ever-present morning fog along the Kanawha River as our now wheezing steamer felt its way cautiously back into the Cedar Grove yards with the profits of yet another night's gleanings from the coal spurs, a night somewhat more adventurous than normal, one would hope.

Slogans and catchy phrases emblazoned on rolling stock were not the lot of the average short line. In fact, the wholly owned rolling stock on which to display such advertisements was often a rarity in this world of secondhand equipment and make-do maintenance. However, the Bevier and Southern, a coal-hauling shortline in north central Missouri, went at least part way with a somewhat conservative and literal "have train — will haul" added to its motive power identification.

Better known by last-ditch steam admirers, though, was the road's use of two leased Burlington 2-8-2 types all through the early stages of the demise of steam, creating a sort of steam haven for a number of years. Here one of the carrier's own Moguls wrestles 15 coal-filled gondolas out of the strip mines and up to the line's single connection with the Burlington's main at Bevier, the home terminal.

266

At right At the time of this exposure, August of 1948, the Buffalo, Union-Carolina, a mixed daily affair in deepest South Carolina, possessed two locomotives, but only one tender. More in keeping with the other 50% of the roster — which was a switching-duty machine — the short, slope-deck tender adds a rather bobtailed look to green-painted Ten-Wheeler No. 3 as it hastens into Monarch, S.C., with the daily mixed. (—*H. Reid*)

Below "Sentenced to the rock pile for the remainder of your natural days." And thus confined, Ten-Wheeler No. 7802 toils in the quarry near Graniteville, Mo., and muses upon her fate. Her ancestry obvious to students of Missouri Pacific steam power, the tall-stacked little 4-6-0 once hauled the best of them on the Mo Pac's iron but now only sees her successors from a distance while shoving the heavy cars of hard granite onto the interchange tracks. (—*Johnnie Gray*)

Once more commonly found in quarries and private industrial yards, where compactness and economy of clearance are at a premium, saddle-tank locomotives were almost never seen on a daily mixed run. Almost, except on the Nelson & Albermarle Railway. These 2-6-2Ts had no tenders and carried their fuel in a coal bunker, which was part of the cab itself, while their water was in tanks folded over the boiler housing for added traction. A pilot and headlight were mounted on the bunker, since the engines were never turned and half the time proceeded backwards. Asked for a show of smoke while puttering around the sidings at Esmont, Va., where the little line connects with the Chesapeake and Ohio, the craggy-featured hogger of saddle tanker No. 9 obliged photographer Reid with a pall of soot that blackened the landscape and for a time threatened to hide the engine and train from all attempts at photography. (—*H. Reid*)

Below Assuming the time-honored and accepted stance of a century of hostlers, the fireman of the Duluth and Northeastern's No. 14 puts his weight on the water spout in the pulpwood carrier's home terminus at Cloquet, Minn. The businesslike 2-8-0 is being readied for a day's work that will see it journeying to the interchange with the Duluth, Missabe and Iron Range at Saginaw Junction for a fair-sized train of pulpwood loads. After returning to Cloquet with this cargo the Consolidation will spend the remainder of the day switching loads and empties in the giant paper-mill yards nearby.

An Indiana shortline in full bloom. Louisville, New Albany and Cory-
don's daily-except-Sunday mixed rolls sedately and smokily into Cory-
don Junction for a planned meet with the Southern's morning train.
(—*Jack Fravert*)

"Jawn Henry" would be proud to witness a scene such as this. A mammoth C.&O. Allegheny type articulated, with tidewater-bound coal, charges thunderously out of Big Bend Tunnel, sight of the steel-driving man's muscular feat near Talcott, W.Va. (—*Charles Kerrigan*)

19. East of West-by-"Gawd" Virginia

That section of the eastern United States extending from Chesapeake Bay up the James River, over the backbone of the Blue Ridge and into the Allegheny deepness of West Virginia, is a rough-hewn land of wooded ravines and dense morning fog, and its railroads follow the tidewater from Hampton Roads to the Pocahontas coal country. Neither southern nor eastern in aspect, the carriers winding down from the mountain fastnesses onto the tidelands were and are an entity of their own. That triumvirate of Pocahontas coal haulers, the Chesapeake and Ohio, the Norfolk and Western and the Virginian, all perpetuate the general Hatfield-McCoy rule of the region, "stranger beware," tolerating little intrusion by other carriers into their mountain domain, except for a feeble feeler of the otherwise haughty New York Central that extends into Deepwater, West Virginia — with the Virginian's consent at that!

The Western Maryland, although not of the triune, managed to probe into the West Virginia coal country some miles distant from the conveyor-belt rumblings of the big three, and as such the W.M. sat on the edge of the area, neither fully eastern and yet definitely not of the Pocahontas strain.

Once out of the mountain shadows and running for the tidewater ports, the mountain maulers sparred with a number of carriers bound north from Florida and Dixie in general to Richmond and Washington. Mixed with the lumbering Mallets of the coal haulers were the classic lines of the Richmond, Fredericksburg and Potomac's General and Governor class 4-8-4s; the austere yet graceful lines of the Seaboard Air Line's relatively unknown roster; and the green-and-gold of the Southern itself, making its way directly into the D.C. area.

A virtual grab bag of steam-power contrasts existed in this wedge of likewise contrasting topography. Locomotives of extraordinary weight and power roamed the Pocahontas region, where their greatest mission in life was to tote the fossil fuel of West Virginia over the Blue Ridge to tidewater and return with empties. To this end the C.&O. and N.&W. conceived and operated some of the most impressively muscular designs ever to take slack out of a mile of loaded hoppers. The C.&O. indulged in different wheel arrangements with great abandon, eventually operating more different types than any other railroad, running the gamut from 2-8-0s to 2-10-4s, 4-6-0s to 4-8-4s, culminating in a mass of Mallet articulateds and the design that will forever be the road's corporate image to steam admirers, the mighty 2-6-6-6 Allegheny.

The Norfolk and Western on the other hand never veered from the principle of articulation for road freight power and scheduled its mainline hauls behind the reliable big three of the road's own design: the J class 4-8-4 for passenger work; the dual-service A class 2-6-6-4; and, more well known and numerous, the gutty, pounding, low-drivered Y-6 compound 2-8-8-2.

The Virginian, more content with copying indiscriminately from either competitor, operated 2-8-4s and 2-6-6-6s alike, albeit in considerably reduced numbers. At the same time, it maintained catenary west of Roanoke into the mountains, and under its wires rolled 110-ton capacity hoppers in long trains behind the most powerful electric locomotives ever built. The Western Maryland's roster was limited in wheel arrangements but made up for any deficiencies with a flair for red-and-gold striped tenders, freshly graphited smokeboxes and a spit-and-polish look generally absent on other coal haulers.

With such an assortment of engines and backgrounds, steam railroad photography should have been the proverbial breeze. Quite the contrary, however. Poor roads or none at all, hill-country natives who regarded a photographer as a trespasser, and the continual fog and rain-sodden skies all contrived to foil quality recordings. The smog and air-fouling exhausts from the chemical plants of the Kanawha River Valley, a haven for such operations east of Charleston, West Virginia, could alone cancel out quality photography for hours after sunrise each day. Those who infiltrated the area with success are to be commended for their perseverance. Those who stayed closer to tidewater fared better, though the omnipresent humidity is always apparent in photographs taken there.

Tidewater trekkers were not numerous, and H. Reid (pronounce that "Aitch" Reid, if you please) and August A. Thieme, Jr., were the most active of the lot. With more than one publication of merit to his credit, H. Reid has probably covered the area better than any other photographer, traveling on foot, by thumb, by train and by auto. Ironically, out of the vast array of impressive steam once at hand, his favorite was the Virginian's flat-faced, low-drivered 2-8-2s.

The youngest and smallest of the Pocahontas threesome, and perhaps still somewhat bitter after its endeavors with compound 2-10-10-2s in the 1920s, the Virginian was quite content to benefit from the experience and blueprints of its neighbors, copying indiscriminately whatever looked good, although in smaller quantities. A virtual carbon copy of the Chesapeake and Ohio's K-4 Kanawhas, 2-8-4 No. 509 hustles westbound freight through sand and pines near Suffolk, Va. (—H. Reid)

Compared with the C.&O. or N.&W., the Virginian, in this photographer's opinion, offered the least accessible main line in its rural regions. East from Roanoke the line plays hide-and-seek in the low sand hills, appearing intermittently as it crosses the relatively few earthen roads. West of Roanoke, while the highways play tag with the N.&W. right of way, the Virginian iron is conspicuously absent.

This view of one of the most powerful electric locomotives ever built, No. 125, taking 110 of the Virginian's own hundred-ton capacity gondolas back to the coal fields, was achieved in a more or less orthodox fashion. The author raced ahead to what appeared to be a location of merit, jounced down a dusty side road and leaped from the car expecting to find the rails within easy reach, only to discover that a fair-sized stream separated him from his quarry. Fortunately, at that dead end in the road there existed a pedestrian walkway suspended by cables, much like those with which the aborigines of deepest Africa bridge river chasms.

The hum of the electric motors was approaching faster than anticipated; so without further ado this naïve tight-rope novice raced out onto the narrow catwalk — then grabbed frantically for support and hung on for life, limb and camera as the deceiving structure swayed, looped and undulated in dizzying gymnastics. After what seemed like hours the uncooperative web settled to a more stable pathway, allowing the author to tiptoe rapidly, but with extreme care, to the far side and the safety of terra firma. It was a close race, but photographer and camera reached their vantage point ahead of the quarry. However, any camera blur in this exposure is not an effect of the train's speed, but more a matter of the heart pounding so fast as to shake the camera.

Above The big three of the Norfolk & Western line up for an official portrait. The backbone of N.&W. motive power in its last decades of steam operations — a J class Northern, a Class A 2-6-6-4, and a Y class 2-8-8-2, left to right — these types were the carrier's and the steam lover's last hope against the diesel dreadnaught. *(Norfolk and Western)*

At left It was a rare day when Ole Sol shone through the Kanawha mists this brightly. C.&O. K-4 No. 2736 starts 80 empties down the Kanawha Valley, bound for Appalachia, Va., from the assembly yards at Handley, W.Va. Known as Big Mikes to the crews, Kanawha types to the management and Berkshires according to the Whyte system of locomotive identification, the 90 big engines spent a large part of their relatively short lives (1943-52) in this continuing cycle of hauling loads off the mountain branches to classification points at Handley and Russell, Ky., and returning with the empties.

275

What Cheyenne was to Sherman Hill, so Clifton Forge, Va., was to the Chesapeake and Ohio's grade over the Alleghenies. At the bottom of the climb over the 2,072-foot mountain summit, westbound trains exchanged their lighter road power from the sea-level eastern divisions for something brawnier; during the C.&O.'s finest days in steam that meant the formidable 2-6-6-6 articulateds, often in multiples. Appropriately labeled Allegheny types, they were the heaviest, most powerful six-coupled articulateds ever built, and a brand-new wheel arrangement at that. The largest engine ever to emerge from Lima Locomotive's erecting halls, they were the height of the builder's superpower theory of steam locomotive design.

The very first Allegheny type on the system, No. 1600, waits on the switch leads while, with rods flailing and sanders opened wide, No. 1617 comes clawing out of the Clifton Forge yards on the inside iron with 105 cars of westbound mixed manifest.

Specifically designed for the short but stiff 80-mile Allegheny subdivision between Hinton and Clifton Forge, where grades vary from .57% on the west slope to 1.14% on the east, the big Alleghenies ruled this domain until the advent of the diesel. After being displaced by as many as five units of diesel power on the head-end, with pushers to boot, the imposing steam designs appeared from Hinton all the way west to Toledo, Ohio, before their final retirement. (*—Charles Kerrigan*)

276

In the dusk of steam's reign on the Allegheny grades, a simple articulated of the same name puts 110,200 pounds of tractive force to the rear of a 142-car coal drag on the upgrade out of Hinton, W.Va. Quite sensibly, in view of this mass of power, the relatively tiny caboose is safely tucked behind the behemoth's towering tender. (—*Charles Kerrigan*)

A bird's-eye view of a famous coal hauler — moving both coal and people in this case. Two of the Norfolk and Western's famous trio of Roanoke-created steam giants perform in the same manner for which they were designed. Y-6b 2-8-8-2 No. 2129 rolls ponderously westward out of Roanoke toward the Pocahontas coal fields with 146 empty hoppers in the increasing parade of loads down to tidewater and empties back uphill to the mines.

At left the queen of the N.&W.'s justifiably famous steam fleet, J class 4-8-4 No. 602, makes light work of wheeling the seven-car *Powhatan Arrow* through Iaeger, W.Va. Exerting a tractive effort far in excess of many Northern types designed for freight service, the Js were designed to handle passenger hauls, of whatever length was deemed appropriate, without resorting to double-heading. For this feat their relatively low, 70-inch drive wheels were a wise design choice, and yet they could whip the same train into a 100-an-hour gait with little more effort. Aesthetically and mechanically they were a tribute to their designers. (*—Charles Kerrigan*)

279

The 2-6-6-4 wheel arrangement attained its greatest success and most of its publicity in the Norfolk and Western's fleet of 40 such locomotives, but what the Pocahontas carrier used best it neither created nor monopolized. The little Pittsburgh and West Virginia, a 138-mile freight-only line in Ohio and western Pennsylvania, originated the type in 1934 with a Baldwin-built fleet of six locomotives. The Seaboard Air Line helped propogate the species in 1935-37, ordering ten of the machines, and in 1947 the Baltimore and Ohio, still steam-minded, purchased the Seaboard units and put them to work wheeling manifest freight on the Cumberland-Brunswick, Md., division until they were scrapped in 1953.

Published views of these machines in action have been rare; so credit is due the photographer for recording No. 7704 of the B.&O. as it bursts fuming and frothing from Carrother's Tunnel, east of Little Cacapon, W. Va., with westbound freight in 1949. (*—Wayne Brumbaugh*)

What a fearsome beast thou seemest! Behind that formidable facade of dual air compressors and billowing smoke lurks a 1924 U.S.R.A. light Mikado, making a grand show of moving an extra freight south from Richmond, Va., on Seaboard Air Line rails in 1947. (*—August A. Thieme, Jr.*)

Between Jefferson Davis' former Confederate capital at Richmond and the nation's capital at Washington, D.C., the Richmond, Fredericksburg & Potomac — titled, appropriately enough, the Capital Cities Route — forwarded vacationers returning north on the Atlantic Coast and Seaboard Air Lines, or sun seekers heading south from Gotham City behind GG-1s of the Pennsylvania. A true bridge route, the R.F.&P. originated almost none of its own traffic; through, fast limiteds with pleasurably imaginative names like *Orange Blossom Special, Havana Special, Palmetto Special* and *Sunland* were the rule.

Here, the *Vacationeer,* leaves the Richmond terminal for New York and Boston behind No. 611, the GOVERNOR WILLIAM SMITH, one of the road's flamboyantly lettered and striped 4-8-4s named for onetime generals, governors and prominent Virginians, an honored custom revived by the R.F.&P. with the delivery of these handsome engines in 1942. (—*August A. Thieme, Jr.*)

282

Under the shadow of Black Mountain near Appalachia, Va., a 2-6-6-2 with white-trimmed running boards makes loud stack talk, taking a train of coal loads out of the mine country to the N.&W. connection at Norton. The low-numbered articulated with the large number plate belongs to the Interstate Railway, a coal-hauling short line of intriguing operations which in steam days possessed a varied roster of secondhand Pennsylvania 2-8-0s, minute Consolidations of questionable ancestry and several svelte little Mallets similar to No. 23 pictured here. (*—H. Reid*)

WESTERN MARYLAND

As heavy-duty, first-class railroads of the East measure up, the Western Maryland seems to fall far short. The line is closely paralleled for virtually its entire length by the big B.&O., whose double track extends all the way to Chicago and St. Louis, while Western Maryland rails drop behind on the first lap across the West Virginia mountains. The carrier's onetime roster of steam power was a relatively unpretentious assemblage of Consolidations, Decapods and, in later years, a dozen each of Northerns and Challengers. The very nature of its off-the-beaten-path route precluded the high-wheeled Hudson or Mountain types of traditional design. And yet, rare is the steam-locomotive admirer whose eyes do not sparkle at the mention of the railroad's name. The author admits to having felt the same admiration for W.M. power, likening the infatuation to his own inbred love for the onetime steam power on the Frisco Lines of his native locale. The Western Maryland had the same flair for red-and-gold trim and spit-and-polish maintenance, and in an area where restrictive clearances and hard coal tended to produce machines of a more or less regimented appearance the fast freight line stood out as a nonconformist with greatly individualistic locomotives. Something akin to the American trait of independence may have been recognizable in their brawny yet distinguished lines. These locomotives were highly photogenic from any angle and yet have not been photographed enough, as this sampling should prove.

Western Maryland joined the ranks of 4-8-4 operators rather late in the years of steam — late enough that diesel cab units were already on the property in appreciable numbers. The W.M. titled its 4-8-4s Potomacs, in honor of the river that the road's iron parallels for much of its length. The twelve engines of the group were delivered in 1947, and while considerably different from traditional appearance, their look was unmistakably all Western Maryland. The snowplow-shaped pilot, high-mounted headlamp and bell, double sand domes of generous capacity and 69-inch drive wheels, relatively low for a 4-8-4, would have raised eyebrows on any other road.

At left Potomac No. 1406 bursts out of Ridgely Tunnel and onto the Potomac River Bridge at South Cumberland, Md., with 83 cars of eastbound early-morning hotshot WM-2. *(Robert Collins)*

Above Definitely not in the *Twentieth Century Limited's* class, but almost as well known to aficionados of the American passenger train, were the spotless varnish runs of the Western Maryland. True locals they were, where the locomotive was never so many cars ahead that its exhaust could not filter back to lull the dozing rider; nor was the schedule so hurried that the conductor could not pause at one's seat to joke about the weather or the fishing. A trip through the gorges of West Virginia and along the banks of the Potomac behind a jaunty and well-scrubbed 4-6-2, as pictured here, was a day to savor.

K-4 No. 209 steps along right smartly with the abbreviated consist of No. 10 shortly after sunup on a run that will put it into Baltimore by five that evening. This nostalgic action was lensed near Thomas, W.Va., by the dean of Rocky Mountain railroad photographers, Richard Kindig.

Opposite Helmstedder's Curve, ten miles out of Cumberland, Md., on the Connellsville, Pa., extension, was probably the most photographed location on the Western Maryland. Topography, track arrangement and a gradient requiring the use of motive power in multiples combined to make it a rail photographer's dream come true. Here a gutty, big-boilered Decapod cants to the curve with tonnage, while a roaring, flailing, red-and-gold trimmed Challenger lunges at the tail end — all of this within the sweep of an eye.

Nearly all of this is gone today. The raging steamers have followed the dinosaur, and the knife-edge ballasted, double-track right of way is now a single-track, centrally controlled bend flexing to the tread of traction-motored hood units. (—*Robert Collins*)

Below Admirable head-end business and a watering have detained green-and-gold Southern Railway PS-4 No. 1382 at Danville, Va., on a humid day in August, 1947.

Forty-four years earlier another Southern train, No. 97, the *Fast Mail*, made an unscheduled stop at Danville with considerably more violence. On September 27, 1903, engine No. 1102 and her crew were trying to make up time with the mail when the whole train left the rails at high speed, just as the engine headed out on to the high trestle over Cherrystone Creek. The ensuing carnage gave rise to the ballad "The Wreck of Ole 97," second only to "Casey Jones" as the foremost railroading contribution to American folklore. (—*H. Reid*)

The hogger lubricating his charge appears as a ghostlike apparition in this time study. One of the biggest of the Missouri Pacific's renowned fleet of 4-8-2 locomotives sits beside the umbrella sheds of the St. Louis Union Station as it waits for an endless parade of express and mail-laden baggage carts to be emptied into its lengthy consist of R.P.O., baggage and express cars. The train is No. 9, the *Southerner*, with a midnight departure for Memphis, New Orleans and Texas terminals, and the big Mountain type on the head end was once a standard-bearer in steam for the Mo Pac. Its stack exhaust a familiar echo in the limestone cuts through Piedmont, Tip Top and Iron Mountain, the robust Alco-built machine and others of the series were for two decades the road's mainstay in forwarding the heavyweight opulence of the *Sunshine Special*, the *Texan*, the *Hot Springs Special* and the *Texas Mail* over the Ozark grades. (—*Donald Sims*)

288

20. *Everyone Had a Favorite*

For this obsessed and addicted worshiper of steam that favorite was the roster of the Missouri Pacific and all its affiliated subsidiaries. The author offers no apology for a perhaps heavier than usual allotment of space to this midwestern carrier, but then, wouldn't we all treat our favorite with the same respect? Bear with the writer in this — a sort of personal achievement, so to speak — a fitting and proper pictorial recording of the varied and highly aesthetic wheel arrangements once enhancing the firm's 7,000-mile network of rails radiating from St. Louis to the eastern foothills of Colorado, the ricefields of Arkansas, the swamps of Louisiana and, at its farthest reaches, the southern tip of Texas, smack against old Mexico.

It is entirely conceivable that this favoritism had its beginnings with the coincidental flowering of the author's obsession for railroad photography in general. The seed of this desire was implanted by a camera of limited ability, won from a punchboard in the year 1940. Following the initial burst of enthusiasm for exposing various friends, both human and bestial, to film, the desire for subjects more challenging and commensurate with new-found talents became imperative. The Missouri Pacific's No. 15, the then *Scenic Limited*, passed within a good stone's throw of home promptly at 2 p.m. each day, and it was decided that a portrait of this might prove of interest. In lieu of an anthropoidal position, standing firm on Mother Earth, a more simian viewpoint, such as balancing on the elevated platform of a near-by block signal, seemed infinitely more intriguing. Accordingly, the author's first photograph of steam in action, a forerunner of thousands since, was taken in the following monumental manner.

At a few minutes to the appointed hour, this naïve innocent climbed somewhat shakily to the top of the signal, which was found to be considerably less steady than it had seemed from the ground. Promptly at 2 p.m. a big Mo Pac 4-8-2 roared around the distant curve and immediately appeared to increase in size, fearfully and surprisingly so! However, like a gunner waiting to see the whites of his enemy's eyes, this photographer squinted unflinchingly through the peepsight at the onrushing apparition. Suddenly it was there! The signal mast swayed dizzily; the thick, black smoke belched up in choking clouds, and complete fear struck. Camera and picture alike forgotten, hands clutching tightly at the ladder rungs, the author waited what seemed like hours until the choking cloud dispersed and the world once again stood still; then this now learned one descended on rubbery legs to terra firma. Fortunately the camera was secured with a cord to his throat or all would have been lost, and yes, there was a photograph all right; all smoke, no train!

During the height of its steam operations the Missouri Pacific could boast of 16 differing wheel arrangements in service, with all but one of these belonging to the two-cylinder category. The road's only venture into the Mallet articulated field, in 1912, left its management with not only a distaste for the twice-multiplied maintenance of such power but also one cantankerous and ugly-as-sin Mallet numbered, and dubbed somewhat less than affectionately, "Old 4000." Ironically though, regardless of the low esteem in which the roundhouse force held this temperamental beast, the engine achieved a special status, as is customary with such singular examples of motive power. Invariably in any discussion of M.P. steam power the query arises: "They had that one ugly-looking Mallet, didn't they?" Whether it is voiced in scorn or simple amazement depends on the listener's viewpoint.

Unfortunately good photographs of this steam-driven hippo in action are virtually nonexistent. Conventionally posed engine views do abound, and something of the engine's operating history may be presumed from the fact that most views show Old 4000 stored on the dead lines at Dupo, Illinois. When not in its seemingly reserved location, the Mallet was usually to be found shoving or pulling interchange drags over the Mississippi River bridgework. On rare occasions Old 4000 ventured beyond the yard limits and put its muscle to work as lead helper on westbound freights over Kirkwood Hill, west of St. Louis. Such occasions were a rare treat for us, then local young rail buffs tied to the area by age and a lack of finances, especially since this was the only example of Mallet articulated power within many a mile. So indeed, even though it lacked for beauty and provided additional work for the roundhouse crew, Old 4000 was still a thing of pleasure to the onlooker.

More in keeping with our steam-oriented memories of the M.P.'s locomotives were the several different classes of singularly well-proportioned Mountain types. The entire group was an extremely photogenic family of machines, from the largest engines on the roster, the American Locomotive Company's 5335-44 series, which throughout the 1930s and into the '40s held down the number-one passenger assignments on the system — at the head end of three sections of the *Sunshine Special* or powering the opulent, once-a-week *City of Mexico* — down to the lower-numbered groups of U.S.R.A. rebuilds and into the rarely photographed 5201-07 series, a small-drivered machine that escaped most cameras by lurking in the humid bayous of the Louisiana back country.

In most cases having a boxcar-sized oil or coal tender, Mo Pac steamers possessed a boiler shape and appliance spacing akin to that of the highly proclaimed U.S.R.A. look (a design that at once placed any engine in the contest for Mr. American steam locomotive), and the company motive-power department made use of any and all available appliances to enhance this basic form. Mammoth Commonwealth swing-gate cast pilots were applied with abandon; Elesco heaters were draped sedately across the smokeboxes or Worthington systems were tucked snugly up against the boiler flanks. Devoid of fancy striping a la the competing Frisco power, but extensively displaying the company name and subsidiary assignment plus the engine number, the M.P.'s locomotives could hardly be mistaken for identity or ownership.

The Mountain types were the Beau Brummels of the roster, by the obvious ruse of being the more well known. However, when mixed in with their system relatives they were hard put to hold their superior position. The motive-power designers of almost all railroads adhered to a practice of perpetuating the designs that had evolved on the drawing boards of their predecessors, sometimes to the extent of creating a monstrously ugly machine, but more often than not improving on the family design. The latter was the case with the Missouri Pacific's draftsmen, and the inherent good taste in the Mountains' lines was carried over to a host of company-designed and rebuilt power, from the Mo Pac's sprightly, high-stepping Ten-Wheelers to lugging Berkshire types and thundering Northerns.

Old 4000 is enjoying one of its better days, having successfully made the St. Louis yards with a transfer drag from Dupo, Ill. The Mo Pac's one and only venture into Mallet articulated power quietly disappeared soon after the end of World War II.

Having just completed a break-in run from the Sedalia, Mo., shops in October of 1939, newly rebuilt Mountain type No. 5321 strikes a commanding and admirable head-on pose for the photographer on the St. Louis engine leads. The very tastefully designed 4-8-2 was one of seven machines converted from a vintage U.S.R.A. design into almost completely new, 75-inch disc-drivered engines, sporting rollerbearings throughout, a solid cast pilot with retractable coupler, a large-capacity tender and Worthington feedwater heaters.

It was a locomotive of this class that "smoked" the author from his perch on that memorable first photographic attempt. (*Robert J. Foster*)

At right East did indeed meet west in the St. Louis Union Station yards. A Mis Pacific 4-8-4, just in from Kansas City with an overnight haul that includes sle and express cars all the way from Los Angeles on the Santa Fe, towers above a Hu type of the New York Central backing down to the platforms for the outbound S Western Limited to New York City.

The discrepancy in size between such power was one of the alluring features of watching at the St. Louis terminal. Eastern engines that had once stirred a nati the Pennsy's K-4's, the B.&O.'s Presidents and the Central's Hudsons — were dw by the huge and well-proportioned Mountains and Northerns of the Missouri P and the Frisco, which themselves were only of intermediate size when one consic the behemoths on the Santa Fe and Union Pacific. A comparison of the two faces tured here reveals a marked similarity of design, lending credence to observations much of the Southwest's steam power carried overtones of the Central look, gon with the boldness. (—*Robert J. Foster*)

Above The biggest, and the last, on the M.P.'s onetime steam roster, N-73 class 4-8-4s Nos. 2201 and 2202 strike a serene pose on a Sunday afternoon, waiting for the hostler to move them to the wash rack for a well-deserved scrub after wheeling redball freights into the St. Louis yards.

Although the Mo Pac wished to acquire new diesel power, the carrier acceded to the War Production Board's request in 1943 that to conserve time and materials it accept a modified version of the Rio Grande M-68. Minus the vestibule cab and vertical Elesco heater of the prototype, these newer machines were aesthetically an improvement, but seldom were they cleaner.

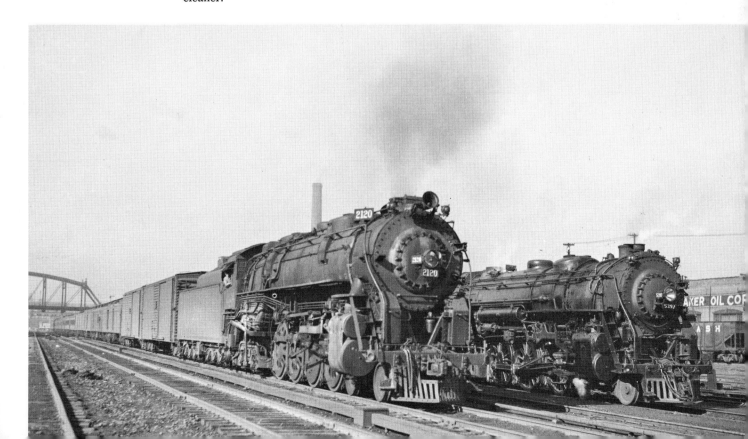

The watermelon crop of lower Arkansas is of world-record size, and when at its peak a specimen could once be obtained locally for as little as five cents. On a hot August day in 1950 the author and a companion procured two such giants in this fashion at Hope, Ark., and left them in the icehouse at Salisaw, Okla., while they investigated the railroading near by. Reclaiming their now frosty treasure at the end of a hot and dusty day, they retired to the shade of the Mo Pac's water tank illustrated here to dine in elegance.

Some 20 glorious, chin-licking minutes later it was only with the greatest effort that these heretofore unbeatable photographers could look up from the carnage of watermelon rinds to watch a big-boilered M.P. 2-8-2 easing up to the water spout. Too contented to even think about scrambling for their cameras, they watched placidly while the Mikado was serviced and then moved on, as No. 1519 does in this scene. (—*Johnnie Gray*)

Little Rock, Ark., is not so far south that the crunch of snow underfoot is an unknown experience. The operator at HH Tower, which guards the crossing of the Rock Island main with the approach tracks to the Union Station platforms, appears to have the feel of it, judging from the well-worn path to the train order rack. A 2-8-2 adds to the already whitened scene as it eases through the plant with a northbound extra headed for the classification yards in North Little Rock. (—*Johnnie Gray*)

Invariably, whenever one of the Mo Pac's sightly 2100 series 4-8-4s is displayed in print its ancestry is lightly touched upon, merely a mention that the engine was converted by the road's own shops at Sedalia, Mo., in 1939-40 from a Lima superpower 2-8-4. Few of the ancestral, 1927-built superpower locomotives have been recorded on film, and what limited photographic record does exist has been supplied for this book by two kindly gentlemen, now in their seventies, Walter Schaffner, a former trolley motorman of the St. Louis lines, and C. E. Prusia, a onetime freight agent for the Illinois Terminal. Both had been very active photgraphically in their home area during the bountiful years of steam.

Above No. 1912 of this rarely photographed group makes a pluperfect wedge of smoky action thundering down the main iron at Eureka, Mo., with westbound redball No. 75 in 1938. (*—C. E. Prusia*)

In an earlier shot, opposite, below, No. 1913 smokes up the Monday laundry in Pacific, Mo., charging west in 1934 with a train of wooden freight cars. (*—Walter Schaffner*) *Opposite, above* Although many of the predecessor 2-8-4s' details were still evident after this conversion, the 4-8-4s were essentially a brand-new locomotive, with a one-piece cast-steel underframe; larger diameter, 75-inch boxpok drivers; a considerably lengthened boiler; and, of course, a four-wheel lead truck. A fast-stepping Northern type of robust proportions was the result.

Carrying the boiler fittings of former Berkshire No. 1902, newly rebuilt 4-8-4 No. 2125 shows the reason for it all, accelerating rapidly through Kirkwood, Mo., with 125 cars of westbound tonnage. (*—Missouri Pacific Lines*)

Considered more appropriate for daily-except-Sunday mixed runs on meandering branch lines than for the head end of roaring mainline limiteds, the Ten-Wheeler type had long been relegated to yeoman service during the period of time covered by this volume. The staple item of motive power on most backwood short lines as well as the mainstay of many a big-city commuter system — and always available for a work train or a local run — the 4-6-0 was used extensively until well after World War II. Missouri Pacific had many of the type in a variety of sizes. International-Great Northern, a wholly owned Texas subsidiary, possessed the beefiest of the lot which it used without hesitation to wheel the finest and heaviest of varnish consists across the undulating Texas topography.

Opposite, top No. 375 rolls out of a sag at 55 an hour near Longview Junction with the eleven heavyweight coaches and Pullmans of No. 1, the west Texas section of the carrier's best, the *Sunshine Special*. (*—A. E. Brown*)

Opposite, bottom Less beefy, and bent on less urgent scheduling, another member of the Ten-Wheeler tribe poses on the armstrong turntable at Kirkwood, Mo., while the conductor and a trainman lean hard on the 6 x 6-inch timber to reverse the engine's direction. No. 2513 is being readied for a morning commuter run from Kirkwood to the downtown terminal at St. Louis. (*—Wayne Leeman*)

Above The sole exception to the backing-in of all trains at the Union Station platforms, this lone remnant was referred to locally as "the plug," "the puddle-jumper" and, in diesel-powered days, as the *Valley Park Eagle*.

As shown here the local was hustled pilot first under the vast train shed. The train's career ended in 1963 behind the drone of an Alco road-unit diesel, to the tune of taps mournfully bleated out at every stop by a bugle-carrying rider of long patronage, while his cronies hoisted glasses high in toast to what had been. (*—Missouri Pacific Lines*)

299

Absent from most hard-bound publications of this nature are photographs of those ever-essential yard goats, without which there would have been no colorful strings of varnish or redball-carded merchandise runs. Grime-encrusted and seldom receiving the attention given to road power, they were always confined within the yard limits, and batting cars down the yard leads or shuffling monotonously from one yard track to another in search of maverick empties.

Considerable imagination and thought — and a lot of luck — were involved in creating a view in which the lowly yard goat was accorded its just due. Soot-coated 0-8-0 No. 9722 has the floor in the M.P.'s vast Dupo, Ill., classification yards as it adds a few more empties to a southbound extra it is building on the outbound leads. Mikado No. 1511 eases up the ladder track in anticipation of the extra's readiness. (—*Missouri Pacific Lines*)

A head-end brakeman on the helper locomotive's tender deck has an intimate view of the road engine on a westbound reefer block as it storms up the east side of Kirkwood Hill, the ruling gradient just west of St. Louis. For some eight miles on the westbound ascent the heavy freights climbed along "the boulevard." This double-tracked stretch of manicured right of way was bordered by well-trimmed grass and neatly clipped hedges, and overlooked by rambling two-story residences of generous fretwork, set well back on shady lawns with gazebos. All this speaks of another era, when there were more finances and more concern for the upkeep of both homes and right of way. (*—Wayne Leeman*)

301

The drama of steam days is evident in this scene of two big J class 2-8-2s of the Louisville and Nashville swinging past HK Tower at Anchorage, Ky. The operator has both delivery hoops at the ready while the fireboy extends his arm for the pickup.

Today's delinquent scene at HK is devoid of tower, operator and steam power: this junction of the L.&N.'s Cincinnati division with the C.&O.'s Lexington division is now governed from a centralized traffic control panel many miles distant. (—Jack Fravert)

21. Orders on the Fly

Alterations in the American railroad scene have not been entirely restricted to motive power alone. The sudden improvement technology that followed in the wake of steam's banishment has caused the comparatively unheralded decay of the once familiar trackside environment through the sterile efficiency of electronically controlled track interlockings, centralized traffic control, train telephones and the rubber-tired mobile station agent. Lineside structures and humanly performed tasks have generally been displaced.

The case for efficiency cannot be argued, if efficiency has indeed been the result of these changes, but for the addicted railroad buff the trackside scene of today is one of desolation. The old, familiar signal towers and rural depots have fallen under the efficient axe of the home-office accountant. But more importantly, with their elimination has gone the human side of railroading: the clatter of the telegraph key in the agent's bay-windowed station office, the operator in the old two-story frame tower at the edge of town who laboriously levered switches and signals to guide the oncoming trains. Both of these men were the connection between a fixed location and the fast-moving passenger trains and redball freights hurrying nonstop toward distant destinations. Before the advent of today's communication marvels these agents were a key link in the train dispatcher's sometimes frantic attempts to keep the trains moving without delay and without collision.

The main weapon in the dispatcher's strategy was the written train order, conceived by the dispatcher many miles distant, delivered by telegraph to the agent at trackside, who in turn delivered written instructions to the head and rear-end crews of the specified train — without slowing or stopping it. Woe betide the operator who forced the limited to a stop for these written orders. Delivered "on the fly" by means of a retrievable hoop, or on loops of twine through which a calculating fireman could thrust his arm to snare the missive, the "19" orders as they were known were often transmitted to the operator by a harried dispatcher just as the train hove into view. The operator then had to copy the instructions, read them back for safety, entwine them in the fork of the delivery hoop and rush out the door to within a few feet of the oncoming, steam-fed monster. It was a dramatic bit of action, affording an alert photographer the chance to record something of the now all-but-vanished human side of railroading.

The order boards in front of the Frisco's Holly Springs, Miss., depot signal "19s on the fly," and the fireman on a fast-moving northbound freight is about to snare the "flimsies" from the trackside delivery stand. A moment later, with twine properly ensnared on his arm, the rear brakeman picks up the rear-end crew's duplicate copies. (—*Johnnie Gray*)

Above and top, right   It looks so easy! A plodding Chicago, Burlington and Quincy 2-8-2 affords a languid pose of the head brakeman about to spear orders from a delivery fork held by the agent at Machens, Mo., on the St. Louis–Kansas City line. *(—Walter Schaffner)*

Compare this deceptively easy action with that in the accompanying photograph, where the fireboy hangs by his thumbnails and with a calculating eyeball homes in on a forkful of "19s" in the agent's hoop, all the while bearing down on the minuscule target at sixty miles an hour. The location is mid-Kansas and the train is a diesel-powered Missouri Pacific green-fruit extra, headed east on a passenger-train schedule. *(—Missouri Pacific Lines)*

Lower right   This one does it the easy way. Hardly moving from his seat cushion in the bay window, the rear shack on a fast-rolling Southern Pacific freight makes a stab for the agent's extended delivery fork. If he misses the target it will mean pulling the air to halt the train and backing up for the needed message, a time-consuming procedure that would not only bring down the wrath of the conductor and engineer but also ensure an official reprimand. *(—Johnnie Gray)*

22. *A Railroad Fair,*
Would You Believe It?

Fresh and flushed with having just completed ten of the busiest and most lucrative years of their existence, the railroads of the United States decided in 1949 to put on a public display to celebrate the event and show both their past history and hopes for the future. Held on the Chicago lake front, it was a momentous and stirring spectacle. The old and the new were displayed; there were rides on authentic narrow-gauge equipment brought in from the Black Hills of South Dakota; a repeating stage show with live actors and likewise live locomotives played out the many historical events in American railroad history and the affair ended with a showing of the latest in motive power, of which there was plenty. Dual-service 4-8-4s and articulateds had been built in quantity during the previous ten years; the diesel electric had become a reality; and even then the Chesapeake and Ohio's turbines and the Pennsylvania's duplex drives were the talk of professional and amateur railroading circles alike.

For those who witnessed the event it was a memorable experience. However it is not likely to be repeated, for to display once more the shining boilers and polished rod motion of all the modern steam power that paraded out onto the stage would now be impossible, as all have long since been reduced to scrap. At that time, little of this loss was predicted in the spectacles pertaining to the future, otherwise they might perhaps have spurred on a determined effort to record steam before its demise.

At Left Past, present and future all at a glance. Nickel Plate Berkshire No. 779, the Lima Locomotive Works' last steam locomotive and almost the last steamer built in the United States, represented the past and was flanked on the left by what many hoped would be the power of the present and future, Chesapeake and Ohio turbine No. 500. On the right and literally coming up on the outside was the real power of the future, represented by Rock Island diesel electric No. 109. Here was a condensation of motive-power history that only a fair could bring about. (*—Charles Kerrigan*)

THE OVERLEAF

Stack exhaust resounding like gunfire, the abbreviated consist of the *Empire State Express* charges full tilt onto the stage behind the famous No. 999 in a shortened re-enactment of the train's famous speed record of 112.5 miles an hour, performed as far back as 1893. Brief though the re-enactment was, gasps of surprise and excitement from the audience were guaranteed each time old 999 emerged from the wings to show how it was done in the good old days. (*—Charles Ost*)

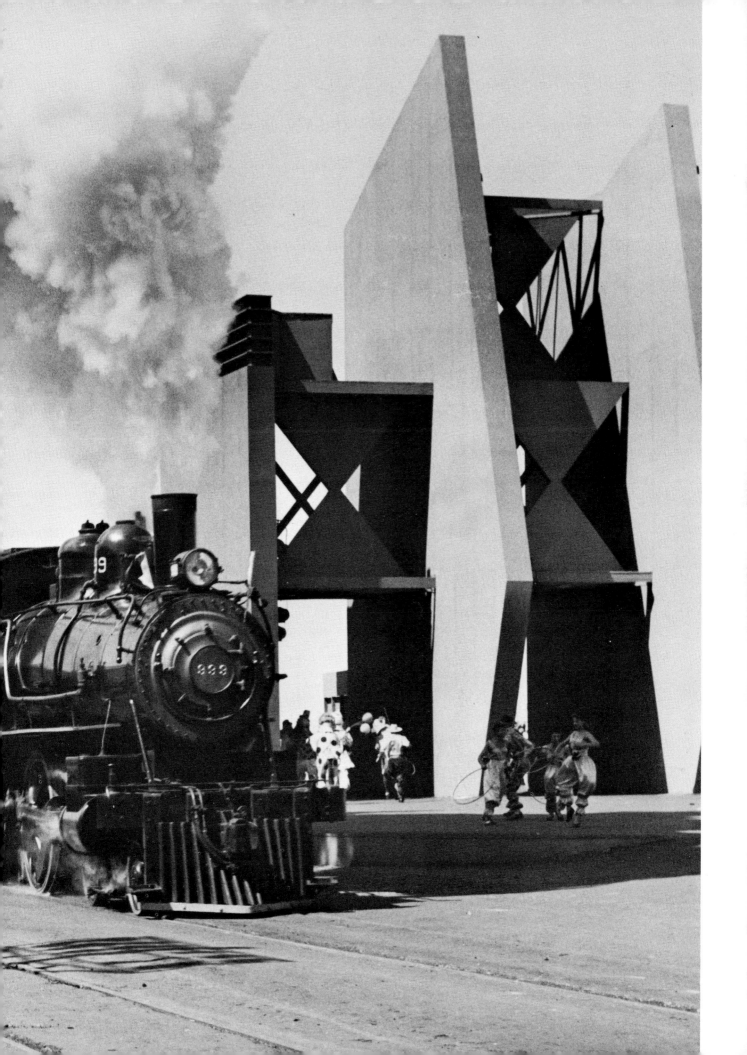

Heading straight into the low-angled sun of early morning, a double-header of high-stepping 4-8-2s rattles the windows of the Attica Junction tower as the lead engine, a secondhand acquisition from the Boston and Maine, slams its pony trucks hard across the intersecting Pennsylvania diamond. Following the ex-B.&M. engine, a true B.&O. Mountain blue blood, one of those converted from a series of 2-8-2s in 1946, and 97 cars of early-morning redball will smash at the steelwork in rapid succession. The speed of all this equipment is made rather apparent, even in a still print, by the nearly vertical position of the rapidly falling home-board semaphore arm, after the two large locomotives and a pair of 50-foot boxcars have already streamed by.

Double-shotted Mountains on freights were so prevalent on this B.&O. division in the mid-1950s that an accompanying rail photographer, after nearly a day of such exhilarating activity, commented with mild disgust, "Cheez, doesn't this outfit ever run anything else?" If only it were so today! (—Walter Peters)

23. *Dawn to Dusk at Attica Junction*

The dot on the road map indicates the town of Siam, Ohio, population 1,000 or under — considerably under in this case — but on the Baltimore and Ohio time-card the name is Attica Junction, a crossing and interchange with the Pennsylvania's single-track Columbus-to-Sandusky branch. This seemingly insignificant dot on the map had its moments of glory in the mid-1950s, when it took on an air of Mecca to the devout Mohammedan. Or, to be more specific, it was a haven for steam-starved souls at a time when one was hard put to find a full day of steam activity anywhere else in the nation.

At first glance looking somewhat desolate on the tabletop terrain of northern Ohio, Attica Junction was anything but desolate in those years. All the traffic the B.&O. could muster on its east-west main line passed here, while the Pennsylvania did its best to pour the entire black innards of the West Virginia and Kentucky coal fields by· in a never-ending procession of bouncing, sagging hoppers. The continual thump of disc and spoke drivers on the junction's ninety-degree diamonds of heavyweight rail was so loud that it drew railfans from far and near.

The tower itself was not to be ignored, although the frequent passage of some of the most impressive steam power in the East doubtless kept many a rail buff from giving it more than a casual glance. It was of standard B.&O. design; two-story frame construction, painted in the company's structure colors — buff yellow with black trim — albeit fading and flaking. The tower itself was becoming as obsolete as the steam locomotives it served. A true rod-and-lever plant it was; its guiding functions were performed solely by the brawn of the operator on duty, and the vagaries of pipe, rods, rollers and elbow bends connected the op's efforts with the maze of switches, derails and signals through which the onrushing tons of steam, steel and freight were routed. While the steam locomotive itself was losing to the onslaught of the diesel electric, facilities like this tower were at the same time losing out to modern, centralized, microwave and automatically actuated train-control methods. And so, on this particular photographers' holiday, both the machines in motion and the lighthouse they passed were contemplated and preserved in memory, and more importantly, on film.

In view of all these incentives it is no wonder that in midsummer of 1956 our artist with a camera — in this case a quiet, unassuming photographer named Walter Peters of Springfield, Illinois — joined the throng of worshipers at this altar to a passing era. It is conceivable that he was also attracted by the twelve big and brawny Santa Fe Railway 2-10-4 types leased by the Pennsylvania in 1956 for exclusive use on this branch, augmenting the overworked remnants of the Pennsy's own once great fleet of J-1 Texas types. Let us witness a day's activities at Attica Junction, and while admittedly it is impossible to present every train movement recorded that day, what has been presented here is typical both of the once beautiful offerings of Attica Junction and of the superb efforts of photographer Peters' 4 x 5 Graphic.

Standing guard over the 90-degree intersection of heavily traveled iron, it is the tower operator's duty to see that traffic passes the point with little or no delay — and naturally without collision! To avoid such a catastrophic occurrence the signalling controls have several built-in safety interlocks, and if the worst happens and a recalcitrant hogger runs the final signal, there is a derail switch to put him on the ground long before reaching the point of physical contact with another train already on the crossing. So, even though it would appear from these views that such a cataclysmic event is about to occur, rest assured that enough time has elapsed between the passage of the two trains to allow each a safe movement through the junction.

On this page we are looking west from the tower along the double-track B.&O. main as Mountain type No. 5575 bores down on the crossing frogs at a flat 60 an hour under a beautiful plume of smoke, while at upper right one of the leased Santa Fe 2-10-4s, No. 5028, roars menacingly down the Pennsylvania's single-track iron with 110 rocking and swaying empty hoppers that will in seconds rattle the windows of the helpless frame structure that is seemingly caught in the middle between the oncoming trains. (*—Walter Peters*)

Trying for a comeback, a President class Pacific works out its last days in office helping a 4-8-2 party member move tonnage, a rare but not unknown sight at Attica Jct. (—Walter Peters)

Above Here another giant Santa Fe 2-10-4 stretches it-self out on the busy diamond. The thump of those big drivers is a good sound to remember, and it is with a great sadness that we will soon depart this celebrated stand. (*—Walter Peters*)

Below The weather begins to take on a dour aspect, just as Santa Fe No. 5026 comes scurrying south with a lone Pennsy N-5b caboose tagging behind, lost in the wake of that gargantuan tender. Evidently more loads are going north than empties are returning south. (*—Walter Peters*)

The seemingly ceaseless parade of double-shotted 4-8-2s is broken. West of Attica Jct. the late-afternoon light was not so weak that another B.&O. double-header couldn't be recorded. Rather than a pair of the Mountains our unappreciative railfan complained about earlier in the day, a brace of heavy-throated 2-10-2s are talking to the world as they thunder east toward the beckoning home board at Attica tower. (—*Walter Peters*)

317

Extra west. T-1 Mountain No. 5593 and 60 loads under an explosive exhaust break the lull between fast-stepping redballs. *(Walter Peters)*

Hooping the 19 orders down — as opposed to the more orthodox method required by the rule book — the tower operator takes advantage of the proximity of the Attica Jct. tower to the Pennsy's rails, a closeness that tends to be unnerving to the uninitiated when a giant like this crusty-faced 2-10-4 looms up out of the mist.

The icebound lakes of northern Wisconsin and Minnesota are just beginning to thaw on this day in early April, 1962, but former Chicago and North Western Z class 2-8-0, now N. de M. No. 1552, could care less. The sun is warm, the track is good and the gringo expects mucho smoke for all the cigars he has passed out. The fat-boilered Consolidation with an equally large headlight, the trademark of all Mexican steampower, is dusting the landscape near Irapuato, Gt., headed for Aguascalientes with a 38-car extra. (—*Fred Sankoff*)

24. Reprieve in Mexico

Desperate for the sight of steam and for the good old days of photographic activity, when steam locomotives were plentiful in the United States, many serious admirers of the machine traveled to lands across our borders for yet one more soul-stirring experience.

By 1960, with steam power largely gone from the operational scene in both the United States and Canada, anyone still seething with photographic ambitions had to turn to the south-of-the-border lands of Mexico where, quite delightfully, one could find both boxpok-drivered Northerns and quaint, squat-boilered, narrow-gauge Consolidations still very much alive and operating in a businesslike manner. It was truly a reprieve from the diesel deprivations of the north. But the irony of it all was that here for many years had existed a paradise of steam-powered operations, overlooked by the photographers because of distance and their loyalty to the familiar U.S. prototypes.

The surprises and pleasures were numerous for those who traveled to the Valle de Mexico enginehouse stalls near Mexico City, to the shops of Aguascalientes or to other still-smoking citadels of unadulterated steam in this land of leisurely attitudes. Here was a sort of retirement home for profiles once familiar to several areas of the United States. Despite the boldface graphics of "N. de M." or personalized embellishments in the form of fancy paint trim, sculptural adornments and smokebox-sized stars more representative of a czarist regime, the old designs were all too familiar. The practiced eye could readily perceive that seldom-mistaken U.S.R.A. look in the boiler of an ex-Nickel Plate 2-8-2, the overly large smokebox door and compact oil-type tender of a Florida East Coast 4-8-2, or the bulky feel of a Zulu class 2-8-0 warming up in the Mexican sun after years of bucking snow and ice on the Chicago and North Western.

To Mexico the photographers came, serious and determined, and their tales of pursuing the iron horse in this new environment were wondrous to hear. Reminiscent of personal experiences with the water in the Rio Grande depot at Chama, New Mexico, were the tales of bad water taken innocently and its lingering after-effects, which for those of weaker stomachs could cancel out for days all activities save those of a natural reaction. Unbelievable were the tales of renting a taxi and driver for a week or more for the trivial sum of $5 a day, and how the determined photographer cajoled, threatened, begged and further bribed the driver to continue what seemed to be an association with the devil himself in the chase across desert and mountain. Never mind that the taxi was a machine some 35 years old, held together with baling wire and ingenuity born of necessity, and smoking as profusely as the steamers it was forced to keep pace with; it was home in a strange land and its driver in time became a translator and a man Friday for the wild-eyed gringo, either arranging smoke effects with the railroad head-end crew or locating a night's lodging at Mama Martinez's in the next village. Generally the Mexican railroad authorities and crews were tolerant and cooperative.

As with all good things, by the time of steam's final hours in Mexico the cost of daily taxi rental had risen 500 per cent — both occurrences in keeping with the times.

Were it not for the generous-sized smokebox door, this one might slip by as a genuine product of Mexico, but that distinguishing mark, plus the compact oil tender, is a dead give away. N. de M. No. 3307 was once a member of that proud fleet of Flagler System, Florida East Coast, race horses. The still very active 4-8-2 is wheeling a 21-car San Juan del Rio extra through a tunnel near Licherea, D.F. The train itself, relatively brief by U.S. standards but of a generally accepted length in Mexico, consists wholly of standard 40-foot boxcars, a sight that even in April, 1962, was fast becoming a rarity north of the border, as rare perhaps as the straw-hatted trackwalker with spike maul and serape. (*—Fred Sankoff*)

Could any other machine be so completely enchanting? (—*Charles Felstead*)

Reminiscent of the egotistically embellished motive power of a czarist regime, a QR-1 Niagara class 4-8-4 of N. de M. actually displays the decorative talents of the roundhouse force at Valle de Mexico. Such colorful adornments, long since passé and frowned upon by the operating departments of U.S. roads, were commonplace on Mexican motive power, and both roundhouse and engine crews took personal pride in each machine. The 1946 Baldwin-built Northern makes stack music during siesta time near Irapuato with a 27-car Mexico City-bound extra freight. (—*Fred Sankoff*)

This, in the author's humble opinion, is one of the finest railroad action scenes of all time. Subtle yet contrasting lighting, twisting rails, a rocky escarpment for a natural frame and a backdrop of rugged mountain all serve to heighten the drama and feel of Lehigh Valley time freight JB-5 twisting and turning through the narrows at Mauch Chunk, Pa., behind an imposing 4-8-4. (—*Wayne Brumbaugh*)

25. *With No Apologies*

Here are presented for the reader's pleasure a grouping of photographs which have all appeared at various times, either in another hardback publication or in one of the monthly periodicals devoted to railroading, but which warrant preservation once again in print. The author feels that each photographer has captured on film a truly outstanding scene of steam railroading in action, one that displays the anticipation and the thrill of steam and clashing steel in the passage of the only machine man has devised that makes his pulse beat faster. These are such commendable works that they should be brought together in a single place for the reader's leisurely appreciation. It is hoped you will agree.

(—Johnnie Gray)

327

Erupting into the clear, cloudless New Mexico sky, a volcanic blast of towering proportions crowns Santa Fe 4-8-4 No. 2925 as it makes slow but steady headway helping four units of diesel power — the first of which emits a weak imitation of the steamer's smoky pillar — in ascending Abo Canyon grade with an eastbound reefer block in 1956. (—*Jim Ehernberger*)

That unmistakable, classic company shot, perhaps the best known of all, appeared on posters, in company publications, A.A.R. bulletins and countless other pages devoted to railroading. The New York Central's L-4b Mohawk No. 3130 scoops water at 40 miles an hour from the track pans in the Hudson River Valley with a wartime oil train in 1942. (—*New York Central System*)

329

Chesapeake and Ohio clearly identifies its bore as Brookville Tunnel, built in '28, out of which exits a very photogenic Greenbriar class 4-8-4, the THOMAS JEFFERSON, with
westbound local passenger No. 93. Brookville Tunnel, near
Afton, Va., at 1,264 feet above sea level is the high point
of the C.&O.'s Blue Ridge Mountain crossing. (*August A.
Thieme, Jr.*)

330

Not too far away as the crow flies, Norfolk and Western's massive compound articulated No. 2037 turns a double-track bore near Welch, W.Va., into a smoking inferno as it shoves hard at the rear of eastbound coal tonnage. The overhead catenary of the N.&W. electrification was still intact in this 1947 scene. (—*Charles Kerrigan*)

Wearing a beard of icicles in the five-below-zero temperature, the Missouri Pacific's robust-boilered Mikado No. 1427 enters Hutchinson, Kans., in a cloud of smoke and steam. Hidden behind all that condensation is the Railway Post Office car and coach of mixed run No. 412, which under more normal conditions rolls behind a light Pacific. On this frigid day in March of 1948, however, the passenger hog remained behind on the main iron, at the Geneseo junction point, to provide much-needed heat for the streamlined *Colorado Eagle*, stalled there because of blizzard conditions further west on the high plains. (*—Richard Wolf*)

A perfect frame of the natural rock tunnel, telltale low-clearance warnings and escaping smoke and steam surround a Delaware, Lackawanna and Western 4-8-4 working hard on the upgrade through Nay Aug Tunnel, east of Scranton, Pa., with first BH-8 westbound freight. (—*Wayne Brumbaugh*)

The funeral cortege convenes. Hideous with intent, shocking in numbers and saddening to think of, the condemned assemble for the last rites. Such scenes as these were commonplace across America during the transition from steam to diesel power. All good-grade steel and iron these beasts, they hadn't long to wait before, with cold bodies and lifeless limbs, they played their own clanking dirge in the procession to the scrap merchants.

(—Below, E. P. Herzog)
(—Bottom, C. E. Prusia)

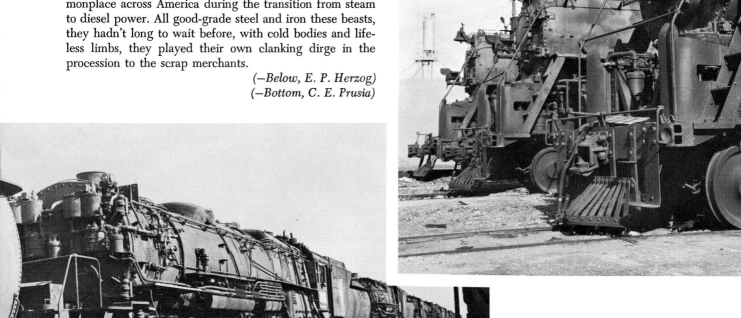

26. The Last Chance

The end had come and gone. For all practical and photographic purposes the steam locomotive was a nonexistent item. Notwithstanding the continual "steam is dead" proclamations of the carriers, complete disappearance of the iron horse was hard to comprehend. Forewarned or not, the fans were stunned. The live, operating, smoke-and-noise steam locomotive was a thing of the not-too-distant past. Total darkness had fallen.

And then a glimmer on the horizon — not a permanent light, mind you, but a temporary brightness — much as the sun's rays will sweep the hills before dipping over the lip of the earth. The railbuffs' special was one last chance to live, smell and see steam before the eternal blackout. Credit them all if you will: the loyal fan; a benevolent railroad management, or one with an eye to making the extra dollar; the promoters; and yes, even the "daisy pickers" — those poor unfortunates who only at the last minute realized that a way of life was about to end. Their only contact with the steam locomotive may have been a paternal grandfather and railroad engineer who sneaked them into his own locomotive cab for a never-to-be-forgotten thrill, or memories of Sunday afternoons spent at the town depot watching the limited thunder by. Or were they just America with too much leisure time on its hands, looking for new and different entertainments? We'll never really know, but what matter? They bought the tickets, filled the cars and made the quotas needed to put the trains on the road once again, albeit temporarily.

Railfan specials were admittedly not new. Clubs, charter groups and even in their weaker moments the railroad managements themselves had sponsored railbuff specials in the years before World War II. The trips were less of a last-ditch effort to experience steam operations than a chance to roam freely over the usually restricted engine terminals with management's blessing or to travel a normally freight-only branch; attendance was usually confined to the very serious students of railroad photography who tolerated little deviation from the accepted norm. They were a far cry from the later excursions' accumulation of heartbroken steam admirers mingling, against their will at times, with those of a shallower interest who came along to show the kids what a steam engine with a passenger train was. Was indeed! One can only wonder if all the newborn infants held up in daddy's arms will ever recall that mysteriously archaic mass of whatever it was.

When witnessed from the side lines, the invectives showered upon the innocents on these later steam excursions were incredibly amusing. Oblivious to the finely focused cameras held in the hands of even more finely attuned photographers striving for the perfect print of whatever steamer was performing on the trip, the naïve were certain to step out in front of the real star of the show, while a boy friend or wife with back to the firing range, ignoring the great obscenities, made instant prints with an instant mortality. As one matronly dowager commented, while waiting for the insipid chime on her instant-print camera, which had just taken an equally insipid pose of her obese companion in front of a Burlington 0-5b's cylinder head at a stop in Galesburg, Illinois; "You'd think the only reason these people came on these trips was to scream and yell at everyone else to get out of their way!"

However little attention they may have paid to the thunderous passage of the steam locomotive in its fullness, the innocent, the naïve, the curious and the interested clamored for these few last brief encounters with the iron horse. The demand was high and the supply short. Those who hadn't even looked up in 1935, 1944 or even in 1950 now looked up as the Burlington's No. 5632 stormed out of Aurora, as doughty little No. 4960 smoked along the edge of the Mississippi, as Canadian National's No. 6218 took water from a firehose at Valparaiso, or as the Union Pacific's No. 8444 smoked up the distant Sherman horizon. They looked up from the coal mines at Reading's No. 2124 — cleaner than it had ever been, and with passenger cars, no less — climbing Shamokin Grade. Those who looked up at green-and-gold No. 4501, a virtual reincarnation of the Southern in steam, looked with regret for not having paid attention to the parade of PS-4s when diesels were unheard of. They'd better look hard; this is it, the last chance.

Grand Trunk Western was the salvation of steam fan trips in the mid-1960s. Just as the Burlington was putting an end to the wanderings of Nos. 5632 and 4960, the Grand Trunk stepped into the breach, using not only its own power but that of other carriers or private parties. The parent Canadian National's 4-8-4s, along with the Reading's own T-1 Northern, hauled the faithful in and out of Chicago over the Trunk's main line east, while Richard Jensen, proud owner of ex-G.T.W. 4-6-2 No. 5629, put his pride and joy through its paces several times on the Trunk's right of way. Only after the inevitably decaying maintenance of this steam power caused several breakdowns out on the main, with consequent headaches for the dispatcher, did Grand Trunk lamentably say no to further steam-powered safaris. For a time, though, the normally obscure and relatively little-publicized Grand Trunk had its heyday as the specials rolled east out of Chicago with almost scheduled regularity.

The Trunk's own 4-8-4 No. 6322 makes a grandstand play hurrying a 16-car special toward Chicago after a day of staged smoke and speed runbys, delays, a breakdown or two and waterings by local town fire departments, all of which have amounted to the usual late return. The well-scrubbed Northern provides a longing last look in the fading light of an autumn day, on the eve of steam's final reprieve. (*—Louis Marre Collection*)

Above Canadians too refused to let the steam locomotive pass into oblivion without appropriate farewell observances. Aged Ten-Wheelers, Mikados and Royal Hudsons all participated in the final salutes to steam.

Royal by decree and regal by virtue of its gray, maroon and gold livery, Hudson No. 2857 wheels a National Railroad Historical Society special into Toronto, Ont., on May 14, 1960. (*—Fred Sankoff*)

Left Ironically arrayed in that condemned "take my picture in front of the engine" pose of latter-day excursions, the typical steam admirers of an earlier day gather alongside a Chicago and Illinois Midland 2-10-2 at Taylorville, Ill., in the late 1930s. Note, if you will, the postcard Kodaks on tripods, the traditional tool of the serious photographer at that date. (*—Walter Peters Collection*)

337

The most beloved sight of all for midwestern railbuffs in the late 1950s and early 1960s was the graphite face of Burlington's 0-5b Northern No. 5632. An alert management, sensing an opportunity for both good will and added revenue, put the 4-8-4 and its distant cousin, 2-8-2 No. 4960, to work heading up fan-club trips, excursions and charter runs throughout the various divisions and branches of the more heavily populated areas of Illinois, Missouri, Iowa and Wisconsin. During the summer months hardly a week end passed without one of these stars being on stage.

Unfortunately, as with all good things, a new management brought an end to these midwestern holidays. Nos.

5632 and 4960 were both transferred to private interests; with the exception of the Mikado, which starred in several Schlitz Brewery-sponsored circus-train outings in Wisconsin, their future was certain only to the extent that they would probably never steam again.

At the height of its public acclaim No. 5632 comes on with a rush and a roar in a staged smoke run for the fans at Burlington, Iowa, in June, 1961. Its 12-car special is headed toward Colorado's narrow-gauge empire for a week of riding behind steam power both big and little. (—Carlyle Shade)

The Northeast came in for its share of fan trips when the Reading instituted its *Iron Horse Rambles* in 1960 behind a pair of T-1 4-8-4s. Reading gave both machines a thorough shopping during the winter of 1959-60; No. 2124 was assigned as a regular engine and No. 2100 as stand-by power. Emerging from these shoppings with aluminum cylinder heads and white-trimmed wheel rims and running boards, the 4-8-4s presented a far different appearance from their workaday garb in coal-train service.

The popularity of the rambles is evidenced by T-1 No. 2124 bending 14 well-filled cars of an outing from Williamsport to Reading, Pa., and return on June 18, 1960. (—*Fred Sankoff*)

340

The Great Western, a sugar-beet carrier of Loveland and Longmont, Colo., played host to many a steam-powered special, usually with the road's singular Decapod, No. 90, doing the head-end honors. However, traditionalists of railroad photography would much prefer recording this photogenic machine as she is here, working under a column of smoke, hustling a load of sugar beets out of Windsor on the afternoon trip to the sugar refinery at Loveland.

Returning from a honeymoon stay at Rocky Mountain National Park in 1960, the author and his unsuspecting bride entered Loveland and were greeted with the blasts of No. 90's whistle as she headed east with empties for a day's work. Quick research revealed that she had been recalled to active service during the fall beet rush. "Nuff said." Days were spent tracking the 2-10-0 in her wan-

derings, and observation soon revealed that the train she headed was indeed a mixed, with provision for passengers in the generously sized caboose.

The agent at Windsor Station could only stare with disbelief when he was asked for tickets for a ride behind No. 90. "My God man, I haven't sold a ticket in 30 years!" was his sputtering comment as he searched the aged desk drawers for pasteboards. Finding none, he exclaimed, "Why not just get on and ride?" But it had become a matter of principal, and a challenge, actually to purchase the tickets. Finally they were located in a dusty bin, where they had long rested. "How far?" was the query; the reply: "The next open depot." "That'll be 20 cents," snapped the now thoroughly amused agent, adding, "It'll cost the company five dollars just to process this!"

In two stirring and emotionally charged exposures, the biggest and best in steam on the Santa Fe plays out a farewell encore to all that used to be on America's longest transcontinental system. Performed on the wide stage of the New Mexico desert under a boundless canopy of azure blue and purest white, it was an arousing exhibition of men and machines at their greatest, although witnessed by considerably less than a full house.

While the ominous undertone of snarling diesel engines pervaded the desert stillness, the star performer played its role to the hilt, thundering mightily and smokily across the stage and into the wings on the horizon, leaving its audience to stand and applaud for one more encore.

It is July of 1956, and in a few hours it will be Santa Fe all the way, without steam. (—both, Jim Ehernberger)

If pleasurable moments could be measured in profits, the D.&R.G.W.'s narrow-gauge remnant across southern Colorado would have turned in more revenue than any other line. The chartered fan-club specials on the three-day Alamosa-Durango-Silverton round trip were usually sold out well in advance, with many ticket holders arriving early by auto to take in the scene of outside-frame 2-8-2s pulling and pushing trains of sway-backed, squat and faded red boxcars. In automobiles and jeeps they followed the panting K class Mikes out of the Chama, N.Mex., yards and into the heights of Cumbres Pass. And the auto road over Cumbres was no interstate: it was graveled, rutted and twisting, and in wet weather as slick as an eel — yet with the fickleness of high-country conditions it could turn bone-dry in the time it takes to put on the tire chains.

For the city dweller on his first safari into narrow-gauge country there was an even greater danger, never fatal but certainly downright embarrassing. Like the poisoned water hole from which the parched hero of soap-opera westerns is about to take his last drink, that blasphemous water cooler in the Chama depot was always temptingly in sight through the open door, inviting the innocent neophyte to slack a thirst long ignored in the heat of the chase. The experienced residents could have voiced a warning, but they smugly preferred to let the unwary drink and suffer. And suffer one did, for the waters of Chama are clear and cool and generously enriched with a tonic of cleanliness.

An oasis of honest, commercial steam operations in a desert of diesel-dominated railroading, the freight runs and occasional fan special with which the Denver and Rio Grande Western plied the three-foot gauge until the mid-1960s were an absolute delight to the steam-starved soul.

Above Looping the loop on a hairpin curve several miles east of Durango, Colo., outside-frame Mikado No. 476 hurries a near last-minute passenger extra over the normally freight-only rails to Alamosa in the mid-1960s. The celebrated and reminiscently opulent private car Nomad follows immediately behind the tender in place of the more familiar head-end revenue express cars of years past.

At right One can almost hear the flanges squeal as this Rio Grande freight follows the curves into the mountains. No. 493, another of the road's elderly but still enthusiastic Mikados, tosses her plume to the sky — and watches it come back down — while assisting with the not-too-lengthy consist.

The hood and the queen. The unrivaled queen of all fan-trip locomotives, an inspiration for thousands who traveled the high plains of Colorado and Wyoming to see her perform, the Union Pacific's great FEF No. 844 shares the Cheyenne engine leads with her most dangerous rival.

The top number in a group of 45 great 4-8-4s that once operated on the Union Pacific's finest schedules, No. 844 (today with an added 4 since a GP-30 diesel usurped her original three-digit number back in 1962) is the only active American 4-8-4 as of this writing. Her exploits on fabled Sherman Hill have made her the living legend of our time. Many a time on the thousand-mile journey from St. Louis to Cheyenne, with little of steam power to inspire him in between, the author has doubted his reason as the hours grew longer and the miles more endless, but the first glimpse of that twin-stacked, elephant-eared, 80-inch drivered machine made it all worthwhile.

Still waiting to receive the third 4 in her number, No. 844 shows her stuff west of Laramie to a trainload of fans on a 1961 Cheyenne-Rawlins excursion. A steam photographer of long standing but an unsuspecting husband of but a few months, the author urged his bride to keep the car even with the fast-stepping Northern — no matter what. And even she stayed, straight through Medicine Bow, Wyo., at 90 miles an hour, much to the surprise of the town lawman, who was obviously so caught off guard as to forego a chase. Her education in the art of train pacing has since been refined.

An anachronism in time but not in locale, the 17-mile Reader Railroad in the possum-trot back country of southern Arkansas was the outstanding common carrier still in steam at the beginning of the 1970s. The snakes and muskrats scatter into the backwaters at least twice a week at the approach of either 2-6-2 No. 108, of Moscow, Camden and St. Augustine parentage, or as exemplified here, former United States Army 2-8-0 No. 1702, whose austere military lines have definitely been improved by artisans of the Reader's piney-woods shops.

As if not content with its steam-only operations, the Reader goes a step further by including in each consist an ex-Milwaukee passenger coach, thus qualifying as the only mixed run yet in steam.

The rather languid flagman pictured here precedes the train to every grade crossing, more to protect the railroad than the roadway traffic, especially since a flatbed tractor-trailer, laden with a bulldozer, nearly annihilated No. 1702 shortly after its first shopping.

Oblivious to the oncoming horde of adoring fans, the head-end crew exchanges a bit of cab gossip while building up steam pressure in No. 844 before another smoke-belching, whistle-pulling trip to Sherman's Summit in 1961.

The display of graphics below the engine number on Union Pacific cab sides, when deciphered, provided a great deal of information about the machine. In this instance the letters "FEF" identify No. 844 as a Northern type (Four-Eight-Four), and the figure "3" declares the engine to be in the third group of 4-8-4s built. The "80" signifies that the engine has 80-inch drivers, while the fraction "25 over 32" refers to the diameter and stroke, respectively, of the cylinders. The figure "266" gives the weight on drivers in thousands of pounds. Were No. 844 coal-fired instead of burning oil, there would have been a letter following the above to identify the stoker type.

Southern salvation, just when the situation seemed the bleakest! The Burlington's No. 5632 sat in a crumbling enginehouse in south Chicago, in a crumbled state herself; the Reading's *Iron Horse Rambles* were only a pleasurable memory; onetime savior Grand Trunk had voiced a final, definite no to further steam specials; and except for a rare appearance of the U.P.'s indomitable No. 8444, steam excursions on big-time carriers appeared to be a thing of the past. And yet, as though each geographic area of the nation must have its chance to rekindle fond memories, the South indeed did rise again! Resplendent in polished apple green and gilt-edged trim, and bearing the gold-leaf herald of that onetime spirit of Dixie, the Southern Railroad, Mikado No. 4501 paraded forth to renew hopes and desires.

A benevolent and sympathetic management proceeded to put No. 4501 through her paces on every segment of the system. With an eye to profits and public relations — but with an act so charitable and nostalgic as to make Jay Gould and his cronies revolve in their graves — the Southern took its prize into every hamlet, loading school children onto its special train for what was undoubtedly the first and perhaps the only train ride of their lives. Worshipers from afar, yearning for yet one more sight and sound of steam, journeyed in force to Dixie.

One of the greatest tributes to this knight in shining green is the very excellent book by David Morgan, devoted exclusively to No. 4501. Its ancestry as an original Southern freight hog, its stint on the coal-hauling Kentucky & Tennessee short line following the Southern's dieselization and its resurrection from the dead line by savior and mentor Paul Merriman are fully described.

Well-dressed and ready for the day's outing, No. 4501, alias the WALTER C. DOVE, steps proudly out of Princeton, Ind., on its midsummer, 1970, run to St. Louis.

Aroused from its Sunday slumber by the greatest event since cousin Beauregard left to join the Army of the Confederacy, the populace of Courtney, Ala., rushes to watch the North Alabama Railroad Club's lovingly polished Consolidation, No. 77, smoke up the town square while club members and the fire department wrestle a pumper's hose onto the tender deck for a much-needed watering of the limited-capacity tank.

After much sweat and toil to restore the jaunty little 2-8-0, the club is making its first public excursion run from Sheffield to Huntsville, Ala., and return over the rails of the Southern in May of 1971. Anything but routine in a year far removed from steam's activities, the trip in itself was an accomplishment of note. The cooperation of local fire departments at five hamlets had to be secured for a supply of ready water, while at both ends of the run sufficient coal and a lift truck had to be procured, all involving much more effort to keep up a head of steam than in the old days.

No. 77's career began on the Jonesboro, Lake City & Eastern, an Arkansas short line of greater ambitions than profits, which was eventually absorbed into the Frisco. With the dieselization of even the Arkansas branch lines, No. 77 and a sister engine, No. 76, were sold to the Mississippian, where they both performed well into the diesel era, until the diesel merchants found even this Mississippi short line. No. 77 again went up for sale and was bought by this hard-working club.

Symbols and servants of a bygone era. As once with the town horse trough, these watering spouts stand parched yet poised, as if searching still for the iron horse that will never return. (—Donald J. Wirth)

As sure as the sun will rise tomorrow, the memory of their goings will endure, fed by those who saw fit to record. (—*Marjorie M. Collias*)

Index of Photographers

---

*Deceased

357

On the great circle of rail that is the Tehachapi Loop, on the grade of the same name in southern California, a robust-boilered cab-forward 4-8-8-2 completes a scene that was as typically Espee as the *Daylight* amidst the orange groves. With the aid of two like pushers the Silurian behemoth hoists a wartime freight east of Los Angeles, bound over the tree-speckled heights. (*—Donald Duke Collection*)

Index of Railroads